The Art of Presence

The Art of Presence

The Poet and
Paradise Lost

by Arnold Stein

UNIVERSITY OF CALIFORNIA PRESS

BERKELEY · LOS ANGELES · LONDON

University of California Press
Berkeley and Los Angeles, California

University of California Press, Ltd.
London, England

ISBN 0-520-02956-9
Library of Congress Catalog Card Number: 75-40668
Printed in the United States of America

To
CHARLES S. SINGLETON
and to the Memory of
DON CAMERON ALLEN

Contents

Acknowledgments

The text I have used for quoting the poetry is *The Complete Poetical Works of John Milton*, edited by Douglas Bush (Boston: Houghton Mifflin, 1965). I am grateful to the publisher for permission to do so. An earlier version of material in Chapter III appeared in *Milton Studies* I. Permission to reprint has been granted by the University of Pittsburgh Press. Some parts of the manuscript have been presented at various academic gatherings: at the University of Pittsburgh, Rice University, York University, Grinnell College, the University of Kentucky, the University of York, Duke University; at a meeting of the Milton Society of America, and of the Renaissance Symposium of Washington, D.C. The printed book has been tempered by these occasions, and I am grateful to my hosts and to my listeners. I owe a special debt to the esteemed Miltonists who read my manuscript for the University of California Press and who questioned liberally. They will notice my efforts in response.

My other debts, of encouragement and critical response, are to old friends, William H. Matchett, Thomas G. Rosenmeyer, and, as ever, Douglas Bush; and to new friends and colleagues, to Avrom Fleishman, who resisted some of my reasoning, to Donald Howard, Stanley Fish, and Hugh Kenner.

In the daily work of writing and rewriting I have enlisted my wife's judgment freely. I mention her helpfulness, not to persuade her, which would be hard to do, nor to contribute to domestic peace, which has its own ways, but merely for my own peace of conscience.

Introduction

The personal presence which Milton formally admits—
overriding the stricter rules derived from classical precedent
and going beyond Italian theory—is that of the poet-prophet,
inspired but humble; blind and suffering from his depriva-
tion, which he is willing to discuss chiefly as a personal
background against which he can reflect his unshaken
confidence in the poem and in the office of the poet; feeling
his years and isolation from better times and places and
voices, but trusting the voice that governs his poem. The man
who lived his other life—who played and quarreled, who refined his thinking, changed, and developed, who regretted
follies, experienced passing doubts, triumphs, and frustra-
tions with mixed feelings and retrospective judgments, and
further judgments, the man who remembered everything and
who was also son, husband, father—has no direct presence in
the poem. Nor has the man in whom the normal endowment
of emotional currents raced full and strong, with, one assumes, the normal crosscurrents. The man he admits is the
dedicated poet, who must himself possess greatness if he is to
describe it. That poet has thought, studied, and mastered his
art, which includes all knowledge men may value. He has, in
the challenging way which can risk and endure the exposure
of sustained literary expression, mastered his own life. At
least, Milton convinces us that he believes this, and believes
that the mastery lives on in the authentic "potency of life" in
books:

> as active as that soule was whose progeny they are;
> nay they do preserve as in a violl the purest efficacie

1

> and extraction of that living intellect that bred
> them. . . . the pretious life-blood of a master spirit,
> imbalm'd and treasur'd up on purpose to a life beyond
> life.[1]

That higher life preserved in the book is not a simple product of divine election; it derives from an "active . . . soule" which, however gifted and dedicated, has put clock and calendar time, work, and discrimination into the achievement of its purpose. If we may believe the poet of *Paradise Lost*, the achievement also requires help, for the mastery of the dedicated poet still contains much that is admittedly "dark" and "low" when he approaches the great theme. "If all be mine," a middle flight may be all that can be hoped for. One believes the gesture to be more than polite or observant of due ritual. He is observant of something real to him, as to the Son, who addresses the Father with a similar ritual of deference, marking limits, ready to apply the personal negative to any separation from ultimate truth, never "too secure" in his own power and mastery.

Whether everything in the poem is finally all the poet's or not—nevertheless, after it has been safely written down and after the always dangerously personal has been transformed, there can be no question of shifting responsibility to the Muse. The principles of freedom do not lack iteration in the poem, and the poet will not plead ignorance of the law, which extends from the word "Of" to "way." One is but emphasizing the obvious to say that the poet is on trial throughout and that he knows it. Insofar as he, and he alone, is to be judged by the moral, intellectual, and artistic choices he has made, the poem is incontrovertibly all his.

The poet's dedication does not prevent a strong sense of his presence in the poem. That is Andrew Marvell's word ("for I saw him strong"), and it suggests doubts arising from the poet's sheer display of power. The boldness of the "vast design," the problems of religious and poetic decorum, the intellectual difficulties in finding the right way through a terrain filled with long-standing human and theological perils, the unflagging energies required and produced, the language to be discovered of sufficient "compass," the finding of materials to "furnish such a vast expense of mind"—all these obstacles to be overcome, though staggering in scope, belong to traditional concepts of poetic art and its highest accomplishments. A blind poet, if he is also a prophet, may succeed in his project. But the strength which first worries Marvell seems to imply a personal expression of will that employs but is not contained by poetic art. The blindness suggests a motive and the analogy of Samson (not Milton's Samson); Marvell's verses waver in their clarity, as if in response to alarm at the spectacle of expressive strength capable of ruining "sacred truths." Marvell does, however, seem to be recognizing a potentially destructive strength, personal in origin, and different from the greater creative strengths which are achieved by the man but are described by reference to the aims and conditions of art.

It is difficult to establish familiar relations with great strength, especially if that strength is not chiefly expressed in bursts which may be accounted inspired or destructive, but is instead present in varied yet constant ways that achieve a character. Even Marvell, who is Milton's friend and is honored by the inclusion of his commendatory poem in the second edition of *Paradise Lost*, observes a careful distance which seems to be more than a ceremony of good manners. Though Marvell moves from "he" to "thou," and admits both uneasiness and relief toward the subject of Milton's personal strength, only one subject of praise takes the form of direct personal tribute without reference to virtues established in the critical canon. Milton has treated "things divine" so that both they and he are preserved "inviolate." And yet, though a personal tribute, and an important one, the acknowledgement goes beyond the rules of art only to find another safe, impersonal reference in the rules of a higher decorum.

Strength as an attribute of character does not allow intimacy or the practice in making distinctions that builds confidence in one's bearings and judgment. A simple test is the ability to anticipate, and Milton is notoriously aloof in this respect, in a settled and constant way that does not depend upon superficial devices that a clever man might learn and deploy. It is hard to gauge his excesses—to know when the vibrations cease, and against which limits, expressing which personal substructures of feeling and which calculated, objective purposes. Readers have not found it difficult to argue that he is on the side of the fallen angels, or that he has subversive plans for God, or that he anticipates the true revolutionary loathing for the perfidy of a counter-revolutionary Satan. His imagination of disorder and destruction may be felt as too authentic to be less than complusive autobiographical revelation, like some awakened volcano emptying itself upon its blooming vineyards and gardens. His intense apprehension of the sensuous and the sensual perplexes, as such things are wont to do. He creates critical dissatisfactions engendered by the unprecedented satisfactions he has created but refused to keep on producing. The range and power of his learning persuade some that he must have learned almost everything from books, almost nothing from life, and nothing at all from acquaintance with the peculiar language of the human heart. The independence and austerity of his mind are such that he may be thought to despise all the more hesitant ways in which men learn to think what they think. Sublimity, oratory, an organ voice, all appear and are remembered, but they tend to cloud and deafen critical judgment. All men are made in the image of God, but only Milton was made in the image of Milton's God.

To a considerable extent the history of the poem is also a history of responses to the poet. The swing of taste against grandeur and heroism, and the acquisition of new bodies of knowledge with their competing claims to wisdom, have naturally produced new ways of conducting the critical skirmishes and the deployment of insight, reasoned learning, assertion, and evasion. The hidden life of the poet in the poem has not escaped notice, and some efforts to identify his individual imaginative life with important developments in the poem have been illuminating. The efforts can also be as whimsical and distorting as less fashionable systems of pursuing literary judgment. There has never been more than a moderate assurance that improved methods can warrant better questions and vice versa, or that new questions will not work up old answers embellished, or that new answers may not flatter the questions and questioners. One may read that Milton "is no longer a vague or unapproachable figure: writers feel that they are facing his problems; critics feel that they can see through him, and round him. . . . There is a new intimacy that goes with this new disrespect."[2] We do not try to remake in our image what no longer interests us, though such interest may not outlast the entertainment of a season, or the discouragement that may come from too revealing a likeness. Milton is fair game, and poets as ambitious as he was to create "a life beyond life" must endure the hazards of the times, as must those who live only one life or write books that are remaindered at once or soon after.

If the "majesty" Marvell praised no longer draws and deters as he said, but may seem to have unusual attraction to the frivolous and profane, others need not prime their devotion to drive off "barbarous dissonance." The poet composing would have been most imprudent if unconcerned with the dangers of feeling "too secure," or of falling like Bellerophon, "Erroneous there to wander and forlorn"; or, the poem but half written, if unconcerned with the dangers of being torn by the mob outside. Once the poem was completed, however, he had no reasonable cause to think that a "savage clamor" might drown his voice.

A chief difficulty of the revived hypothesis that the poet is everywhere in the poem is that one has too much evidence available and too few effective rules for making discriminations. If the poet has already turned himself into the poem, uninspired efforts to reverse the process, without "higher argument" or Muse, but with only prose wits aided by an apparatus assembled for the project, may ruin the poem without salvaging much of literary interest. Reasonable critics, of course, attempt nothing so grandiose, but even they are not immune to some of the distortions and distractions that seem unavoidable.

In addition, a work of such magnitude by a poet of such power may be expected to attract attention that is intellectually ambitious but not directed toward matters of characteristic literary concern. For instance, approaches to the poet may be motivated by modern interests enjoying the use of analytical methods unknown to earlier critics. A major poet controls knowledge in ways that invite efforts to piece together, or search for significant fragments of, the life hidden from the poet himself: in the unexamined assumptions that precede and accompany thought in any age, or in the social forces and historical necessities which influence him directly. These, even when they are resisted, indirectly influence, insofar as an effective opposition is not free to think without regard to the strengths and weaknesses of what is being opposed. One may also mention the modern interest in the hidden life of childhood, with its groping relationships of feeling and necessity which can neither be remembered exactly nor be forgotten quite. The analyst with a theory and a *corpus operum* to sift through may feel qualified to reveal what was concealed to the author. Another hidden life is the one nurtured by the partly hidden life of myth, which may or may not include private sexual representation and may or may not be encoded in the poem.

The sophisticated enterprise of interpreting the work as the poet's projection of psyche—its roots in Romanticism, its executive techniques in the present—raises its own difficulties in the evidence it suppresses, or transposes according to its own code of beliefs. The poet hypothesized as creating by "recreating" himself may remain partly immersed in chaos, deprived of the distinct uses he makes of his human endowments and acquired skills. To subordinate or set aside his active consciousness and detachment, as if they were not present in the imaginative dark that does not disorder, may be risked to gain a particular angle of vision; the results, however, cannot comprehend or substitute for the image and presence of the poet Milton deliberately creates. The "active . . . soule," the "living intellect," though austere and impersonal in concept, exerts unmistakable force and is present in the choices that direct the narrative. The subject is not an obvious one, discredited by intellectual progress; nor is it exhausted by factual references to Milton's known beliefs and intellectual conclusions. We cannot safely ignore the evidence that Milton enjoyed the art of practicing degrees of visibility. The complex character of reticence in the poem, all the silences, delays, interruptions, varieties of balance and imbalance, the unexpected parallels and the unexpected variations of established patterns, the constant of surprise—all master the problems of the story and reflect the author. All no doubt reflect the man behind the author, but only the author is a guiding figure throughout the poem—more elusive and provocative than Dante's Virgil but hardly less present; at moments reminding one of Shakespeare's Prospero, but with many differences.

I have not attempted to compose a full portrait of that figure, which does not offer itself standing still or always looking the same. Not seldom we may feel mocked by the sense that the poet has anticipated our trying to overclarify the separations and identifications of architect and work. Moments that in another poet would be sheer entertainment command study, produce controversy, and may perhaps make some readers feel that they are being dominated by a dazzling genius whose purposes they distrust. Others may wonder at the exuberance of vitality, at the joy in expression that exceeds the personal, honoring only the shared human gifts of response. Even his moral commentaries punctuate and do not simply depart from the story; in their placement and emphasis, or in their absence when we expect them, they do not invite a single, automatic response; nor do the many silences which vary in their duration and in their depth. The subtlety and range of his detachment is a necessary other side of his deep commitment to the truth of the story, and is one valid symbol of the personal equilibrium he achieves as an artist. His conduct is also evidence of his concept of the mastered life present in the poem, on trial but not acting a simple dramatic role.

I have not attempted a full portrait, but some of the items named above will come under further study in the course of the book. We shall find that, though only the presence of the dedicated poet is formally admitted, there are many aspects of presence which are revealed and concealed to satisfy the purposes and the pleasure of the poet's art. This kind of presence is imaginatively varied in what it does and in the degree to which it will submit itself to observation. The blind poet prays for vision. He does not acknowledge but surely demonstrates his uncanny awareness of the responsive presence of his unseen readers, whom he touches with tremendous force and with marvelous lightness.

A few words on the astonishing uses he makes of his voice may serve to suggest still further aspects of his presence. The narrative voice may obtrude deliberately, or seem to flow without a remaining trace into words, descriptions, and actions that present themselves with vivid anonymity, as if speaking themselves. The anonymity possesses considerable range, delicate in its mastery of the fleeting, adapting itself to the exact expression of person and moment, great or small, in movement or stationary, and not without a comic gift for realizing human states of confusion or triviality, nor too fastidious to convey the disgraceful and the vulgar. Like a ghost the voice materializes, in many shapes of personality, and may disappear at once or linger in a tantalizing transition or delayed echo. Criticism has barely begun to study the presence and effects of Milton's voice in the poem.[3]

If the history of the poem is also in part a history of response to the poet, small wonder we find such remarkable items as:

belief in his undeviating gravity, in his having invented everything, or nothing, in his treating all doctrine as myth, in his being a learned victim of his literal adherence to a system of outmoded ideas, in his being incapable of understanding the consequences of his narrative structures, in his incapacity to vary the style, or to visualize, or to hear with discrimination. One could extend the list immensely, but I shall add only one further item that, so far as I know, is not on record: the complaint that Milton cannot be forgiven for having made Adam experience the death of his son Abel not once but twice. This comes from a professional scholar of cultivated sensibility, and it seems worth examining because of the way it identifies the poet and the poem.

The response resembles, at some distance, discussions of what Adam should have done when faced with Eve's apparent resolution to divide their morning's work in the Garden, and such responses honor the story by moving it out of its fictional realm to answer the analogous but not identical obligations of the non-fictional world. *In the story* Adam will see the death of Abel only once, and Milton must take the responsibility for having chosen to make Adam undergo this terrible experience—along with the punishing vision of the future, including the Flood, which, if the poet had decided otherwise, Adam would have been spared in the story, as in life.

A powerful fiction is not likely to promote a state of contemplative admiration in which we are content to enjoy the formal excellences unperturbed. A good story draws us into its conflicts, and into its potential alternatives and extensions. Responses to Milton the man, his subject, and his ways of telling the story as well, may distract us from the kind of profundity in imaginative fiction at its best, which treats the depths and shallows of human nature in expressive conflicts with the shallows and depths of the human condition. Such fiction always invites comparison with the concerns of non-fictional life, but we honor the work most by hearing out the story and by pressing our own urgent questions with a tactful observance of the special rules which may be expected to govern all oracles of wisdom. The poem as fiction is such an oracle. The poet has undertaken a work of great compass and depth, and has not pretended to transmit only a pure dictation, without foreknowledge, or art, or fictional "accommodation" to the intelligence of the reader, or without his own deep but disciplined involvement in both the fiction and the non-fiction of the story. He is therefore answerable to our own deep involvement in the major and minor truths of the story. But as with oracles, or forms of human discourse, or bodies of knowledge, or social or religious structures— impatient or careless questions, indifferent to the known rules and inner spirit governing the knowledge we seek, will return answers that reflect the particular ineptitudes of the questions.

The present climate of critical opinion no longer encourages a simple identification of Milton with Adam's anguished expression of misogyny after the fall, and the swing of opinion may go so far in the opposite direction as to leave the poet entirely out of a dramatic world in which all conflicts are self-balanced on their own axis. These are by no means the only alternatives. Indeed, to speak of the present "climate" of critical opinion is to employ a metaphor which has seen better days, when it could be thought to represent a free and spontaneous harmony of forces in which things might be located and understood—whether by historical scholar or modernist. The present climate is no less free, but its harmony is produced by competing hothouses, forced growth, and altered time schedules. Promising opinions exhaust themselves and are retired to the compost at record speed.

If I take a Burtonian view, swept aloft by that heady air secreted in libraries, I may note various drums and trumpets that have been sounding their overtures. The art of our critical necessities makes the strange familiar, and a surge of new answers continues to require, invent, and employ new questions. The poet can be locked into the poem, and the poem locked again, and only one password will enable the entrance of the faithful reader behind whom the lock fastens. At the other extreme, various kinds of creative demolition may be pursued as poem and poet are taken apart—to show that it can be done, to show other things regarded as valuable, or to recompose the materials into experimental fictions that may providently assert the temper of the times.

For the most part in what follows I shall try to keep some free distance between what I have read about Milton and my own efforts to illuminate issues. Accordingly, I shall not argue against current interpretations which differ from my own judgment of the ways the poet writes himself into the poem. I regret the spare provision for systematic scholarly courtesies, knowing, as I do, that even at the best one never gets all the direct and indirect obligations straight. Besides, one seldom credits properly the half-forgotten suggestions picked up along some apparently uneventful miles of print traversed. Nor is one always an adequate judge of what happens by the immediate and remote leverage of disagreement. I have tried instead to manage my part of what I think of as having been a long conversation with the poet. *Paradise Lost* was and is a great work of the literary imagination. There have been and will continue to be many ways to develop or qualify or oppose the preceding statement. The quarrels among readers, though they produce inordinate slippage and diversion, constitute one of the authentic ways. I have chosen another. Anyone who is interested enough to care should be able to understand why, for instance, I do not regard the poet of *Paradise Lost* as a committed prophet; or as, quite, a self-including dialectician-creator who composes everything, from "one first matter all"; or as, quite, a rigorously self-excluding dialectician.

The questions I address are ones I believe to be vital: both old and new. The categories to which my questions belong were old when Milton was writing. Critics, as Marvell found it useful to do in the scheme of his poem on *Paradise Lost*, divided their attention among the poem, the poesy, and the poet. But I am not defending old or new fashions. I intend to speak as well as I can to modern interests. Andrew Marvell is an encouraging witness, one whose voice carries from then to now with recognizable clarity and force. Another guide to the poem, often in my thoughts but not to be referred to in this way elsewhere, is the figure of Adam, not only unfallen but not yet created: the idea of Adam as Raphael describes "the master work" which is to consummate the sixth day, "the end / Of all yet done." The Creator and the poet collaborate in making an ideal figure at least one range of whose privileged responsibility may instruct an ideal reader of the poem:

> *self-knowing, and from thence*
> *Magnanimous to correspond with heav'n,*
> *But grateful to acknowledge whence his good*
> *Descends.*
>
> *(VII, 510–13)*

That the reader is not in the Garden of Eden, and that the poet is not God, and that Adam and the reader have particular "active spheres assigned"—those differences must all be understood if the comparison is to communicate its shared range of similarity. What the comparison may then tell us is that if one can bring a measure of magnanimity to the poem, the virtue will improve and with it one's capacity to correspond with the poem and its creator. In addition, the more particular privileges of the reader require that he correspond, not with passive acknowledgment but with active response, knowing and self-knowing, inquiring after and judging the purposes, the means, and the human acts of decision that speak through the poem.

And one last introductory statement, which I borrow from a page early in the next chapter. The context is that of trying to imagine Milton's response to Andrew Marvell's commendatory poem. I quote my words here, for they express my own understanding of where this book begins and where it is going: "There could not have been much news here for Milton to read, though that tone of admiring deference, combined with the demonstrated credentials of independent insight and appraisal, must have been gratifying. Prolonged and lonely effort is never quite answered by applause for the beautiful results; only shared insight into the nature of the difficulties confronted and the ways taken to overcome them can speak to the poet in the poem."

I.

Beginnings: Speaking
to the Poet

In *The Prelude* (1805) Wordsworth spoke "of primitive hours" when

> *I experienc'd in myself*
> *Conformity as just as that of old*
> *To the end and written spirit of God's works.*
> *(IV, 348–51)*

The late Earl Wasserman was intrigued by these lines, and we had several animated conversations on their significance and on their probable connections with Milton. I begin this book by offering some comments on lines that record Wordsworth's profoundly personal experience, which Milton must also have felt in his own way while embarked upon his own enterprise. Yet there are individual and historical differences, and some of these endowed Milton's story with a narrative endurance beyond the personal. In quoting Wordsworth I have in mind two streams of traditional thought, which easily converge but also have their own separate ways and histories.

In spite of the official interpretations that assigned to the Old Testament an initial stage in the development of God's providence, thoughtful Christians had good reason to observe and feel some particular losses which, in the general growth and gain, had never been exactly replaced. It was some compensation, no doubt, that the oldest heroes of faith could be claimed as types, anticipating Christ and participating in the relived experience of modern spiritual heirs. Another compensation thoughtfully provided was this: If a modern Christian, in spite of his manifest advantages, discovered inward obstacles impeding those easy paths in a ratified design assuring him of personal salvation, he could still count on the encouraging support of closely knit arguments that explained why these new difficulties were also part of the benevolent design and singled him out for special favor and improved benefits. Nevertheless, a sense of particular losses might still be detected, for the old heroes of faith displayed a privileged grandeur of ease no longer available intact. Even brief intimations, as "of primitive hours," would be felt as precious privilege, intimations of a Golden Age.

This is the first of two streams of traditional thought which Wordsworth's lines suggest. The Garden of Eden provided the most authoritative image of the Golden Age, but some spiritual heroes continued to reside in a personal atmosphere barely removed from that of the original garden.

> *Sweet were the days, when thou didst lodge*
> > *with Lot,*
> *Struggle with Jacob, sit with Gideon,*
> *Advise with Abraham, when thy power could not*
> *Encounter Moses' strong complaints and moan:*
> > *Thy words were then,* Let me alone.
>
> *One might have sought and found thee presently*
> *At some fair oak, or bush, or cave, or well:*
> *"Is my God this way?". . . .*[1]

"Sweet were the days" of simple directness between man and God, the days of natural ease and familiarity.

To a later age equipped with a well-tested apparatus for pronouncing upon such matters, the psychic integrity of the heroes could not but seem remarkable. Indeed, some heroes of faith in a Golden Age seemed to demonstrate affections and will in such easy accord that the normal contributions of reason had little to say, and the protagonists appeared to take for granted what observers could not but wonder at. Ever-vigilant reason, man's highest faculty, enjoyed a mysterious liberation from its duty of assigning phenomena their proper moral place in the universal scheme of things. The old heroes, without the labors of mind expected by a medieval contemplative passing through the prescribed stages of his progress, seemed to be rewarded by their own full sense of intellectual ease and splendid leisure. If their reward lacked the extraordinary privilege of attaining the heights of contemplation, in order to marvel at the manifest evidence of God's greatness, they did, notwithstanding, possess another remarkable gift, that of participating in a lost ease and casual familiarity of address between man and God. One of the subtle privileges of the enlightened mind has been to invent for itself the enjoyment of vision without the normal inconveniences of full citizenship even in a blessed time. Be that as it may, thoughts of the Golden Age lived on in many ways, but especially in the intimations of possible recovery, our present point of concern.

A second stream of thought suggested by Wordsworth's lines more than compensates for the modest emphasis accorded intellectual activities in the experience of heroes of faith. The *records* of authentic beginnings are remembered, always learned by heart in the most primitive sense, and imaginatively returned to, and searched, for the laws governing existence. Beginnings are, in the traditional metaphors, the source and origin, the spring and fountain of the pure. The first impressions left by creating Providence are the visible signs of God's eternal purpose and meaning, "the end and written spirit of God's works," inscribed at once in nature, the soul of man, and sacred writ. When Whitehead, the least dogmatic of metaphysicians, declares that the world can take no holiday from its own first principles,[2] he is not locating the foundation of those principles in a place and time. Priority in time is not a working rule of thought for Whitehead, who is more interested in showing the faults and distortions that arise from assuming that all necessary knowledge is available. Nevertheless, if absolute first principles exist, they must be assumed to exist before—and independent of, though waiting for—the understanding that hopes to discover them, and countless generations of professional thinkers were convinced that the priority principle was an indispensable thread through the labyrinth of thought.

If the ultimate truths were mental, and invisible, philosophy and faith, even when aware of each other, could arrive at similar conclusions independently. No careful theologian exercising his reason in a *summa* would fail to acknowledge that nothing arrived at by his own strenuous methods was intended to surpass or contradict the simple conclusions of inspired faith. The substance of thought consisted of principles and examples. There was no sublunary thinking without an image. Traces of the invisible were there to be discovered in the visible, and the images of likeness were not simple doubles exactly mirroring each other, fixed by the discovering act of observation, but were complex and suggestive likenesses requiring individual interpretation. The assembling action by the syntax of thought was itself a further process of interpretation. Man created in the likeness of God was a master-image, an example that encoded the principles of a philosophical anthropology. By traditional agreement the essential likeness existed in man's intellect, which by its endowment of resemblance could recognize and interpret the visible signs leading to their invisible source; and thus man could govern his thoughts and actions in accordance with the divine precepts.

When Wordsworth experienced just and perfect conformity "To the end and written spirit of God's works," he was in effect uniting example and principle, the visible and the invisible. The "hours" themselves had to be recovered from the freedom of a Golden Age that preceded man's familiar obligation to interpret. To feel at one with creation was to feel entirely at home, and to experience a sober joy that validated the purity of origin. One cannot distinguish between the sense of return as reward and as confirmation; the experience produces an integrity which enjoys the fruits of thought without the cultivation of thought. (A detached observer interpreting an experience that presents itself as unmediated by interpretation may, however, note that chosen emphasis on the felt return, which the traditions of thought would recognize as neither superfluous nor strictly necessary, for the sense of perfect conformity with the order of God's continuing purpose would, at any juncture, touch both beginning and end.) The spirit is invisible but written, inscribed in the products of creation, eternally decreed. The traditional image of "reading" is implied in the experience but requires a correspondence of spirit, with the human discipline of interpretation passing into a spontaneous, unlearned integration, at once retrospective and prospective, momentarily contracting and infinitely expansive. Moments, or hours, or a day, or a thousand years, reflect the truthful small habits of human speech, convenient, like entrance, vestibule, or exit, but not a measure of the experience within. The mention of time in one of its customary partitions only increases the sense of participating in God's undivided time.

But what of Milton, who had all this at his fingertips and could make it sound like an anthem, or could develop the intertwining variations, or touch into life shaded inflections more subtle than these? "Conformity" is a word that he must use warily, for it is stained by the Reformation and Counter-Reformation polemics of the times; he prefers the word "obedience," diamond-hard and dangerous to the purveyors of cosmetic euphemisms. His subject is "man's first dis-obedience," which requires, if God's ways are to be justified and man's ways are to be understood, a prior state of obedi-ence. The poet cannot be diffident toward that part of his narrative obligation, but his story is a long one that cannot be sustained by, cannot take off from, lyric moments of personal discovery. The prior state must affirm what all men have always thought and felt, but Milton has his own ways of uniting, and juxtaposing, principle and example, and he has his own confident sense of timing and pace, and a sublime assurance in the discoverable laws of decorum and in untried principles of architectonics.

The development of his thought in prose requires that one also measure the effects of his immediate obligations in pub-lic debate, and also the effects of matters of timing, and the response to obstacles and opportunities created by the nature of positions already fortified by opponents. Such considera-tions lead away from but do not disturb the simple conclu-sion that his thinking was too long and too deeply committed to issues that involved freedom and the consciousness of freedom for him to give himself entirely, in the masterwork of his maturity, to a large answer valid chiefly in its retro-spective force, an answer that could not speak with moving eloquence to the problems of human destiny and freedom in the present and future. He took the bold and simple position that an essential continuity existed between freedom in the Garden of Eden and in the streets of London.

His theme and his rational beliefs bind him to celebrate the state of innocence, and he aims to provide ample satisfaction, but he has no desire to write a story that will stimulate and water the passions of nostalgia or that will encourage the human propensity to invest idolatrous thoughts in a place or a time. Though he does not register the claim explicitly, the author of *Paradise Lost* is convinced that poetry has an in-spired power to recreate the original state of human perfec-tion. In the formal curriculum that Milton describes, the practice of advanced composition comes late, only after the candidates are qualified by having acquired "an universall insight into things,"[3] and after they have submerged themselves in the study of logic, rhetoric, and poetry. The order of that study is locked in a pregnant ambiguity, a sudden reversal in mid-sentence that seems as fraught with inclusions as with exlusions: first come the heads and topics belonging to the fist of logic, then the gracefully open palm of rhetoric, "To which Poetry would be made subsequent, or indeed rather precedent, as being lesse suttle and fine, but more simple, sensuous, and passionate." In Milton's most austere curriculum, suggested in *Paradise Regained* (IV, 324), one must bring "A spirit and judgment equal or superior" to the books one reads. That principle, translated into milder circumstances, might enable the accomplished student of poetry to discover that he understands logic and rhetoric before he studies them, and that he is therefore free to turn their elementary lessons into advanced mastery. For purposes of practical education, at least, Milton thinks well of logic and rhetoric, but there is little reason to doubt that he believed poetry to include all their powers without being bound to fine-spun demonstrations or self-conscious grace and ornateness.

The fit reader of Milton's poetry will not lack opportunities to exercise his command of logic and rhetoric, or to exercise the power of his own judgment. These matters have not passed undetected. "Error by his own arms is best evinced"—that maxim proposed by Satan and patently ignored by Jesus *(Paradise Regained, IV, 235),* and variously deplored by zealous reformers as a sluice admitting the contamination of pagan thought into the militant church, is one which Milton must make full and subtle use of in deploying the materials of his poem. The intellectual and moral traditions of Christianity have to be satisfied by the argument of the poem, and these provide one convenient means of carrying out the amplification necessary to an epic. No such convenience, however, attends the problem that obedience and innocence precede error and must pass from one state to the other without the kind of standard process that would compromise the validity of the initial state. The state is at once a philosophical premise which must be maintained and a golden moment of human privilege that need not have been but *was* violated, broken, and lost, but not lost to thought and feeling. The state is also, therefore, both a moment of time separate from all subsequent human history and a moment which contains materials crucial for interpreting human destiny. The free possession and loss of innocence, good without evil, remains problematical, a speculative maze of intellectual difficulties which attract, excite, and baffle. Yet the problem resists the normal human answer of withdrawing interest, perhaps because the undiminished longings cannot tear themselves away from a possible source without crippling and rigidifying the human capacity for hope.

In attempting to understand the problems of the poet, one may draw encouragement from the critical praise by Milton's most authoritatively "fit" contemporary reader. Andrew Marvell, first doubting the "intent" and then the "success" of the strong story-teller boldly undertaking "his vast design," points to the danger in finding a poetic way "Through that wide field" of the simple and the complex, and doing so without turning "sacred truths" into mere "fable and old song," without trivializing the plain or compounding the difficult in venturing to explain it. There could not have been much news here for Milton to read, though that tone of admiring deference, combined with the demonstrated credentials of independent insight and appraisal, must have been gratifying. Prolonged and lonely effort is never quite answered by applause for the beautiful results; only shared insight into the nature of the difficulties confronted and the ways taken to overcome them can speak to the poet in the poem.

Though we are not likely to underestimate Milton's personal belief in a state of innocence enjoyed and lost, we shall not find it easy to determine the relations between that belief and his alert consciousness of the ways of evil. Certain ringing declarations are difficult to keep in their place; we may also hestitate at suppressing them too thoroughly. "As therefore the state of man now is; what wisdome can there be to choose, what continence to forbeare, without the knowledge of evill? . . . that which purifies us is triall, and triall is by what is contrary."[4] No one in his right mind will confuse "the state of man now" and the conditions of Paradise; choice and trial are different now, they have to be different, but they cannot be entirely different. There are also the ringing declarations of continuity, of the similar which must be similar but which cannot be entirely the same.

A piece of witty skepticism, like Marvell's "lame faith leads understanding blind," lies within Milton's compass, but only as a kind of peripheral vision. He is resolute on the central subject of man's continuing dignity and the effective competence of intellectual and moral faculties. The optimism is monumental, more than a fabric of memorable expressions, and not to be construed as a stubborn immunity to the lessons of personal and national experience, but the deepening expression of a sensitive man enduring change with no essential alteration of "that season'd life of man, preserv'd and stor'd up in Books."[5] Of the many questions and answers produced by the force of Milton's optimism, one question is at least as troubling as matters of similarity and difference and continuity. It is how to relate belief in an original perfection with belief in a benevolent Providence that not only turns evil into good but seems committed to bettering good. In public argument the ideal of perfection requires a double perspective. The values are grounded in the recovery of an original state, but the motivation is invested in the future. Thus a hortatory image of truth evolving, though in part directed against well-known human faults, produces ususual weight in its positive emphasis: "Truth is compar'd in Scripture to a streaming fountain; if her waters flow not in a perpetuall progression, they sick'n into a muddy pool of conformity and tradition."[6]

When we turn to *Paradise Lost* we find expressions of that positive emphasis which are freely introduced and are not subject to the kinds of reservations we may bring to the context of a public argument. It is not the complex issue of the fortunate fall that I have in mind, but an apparently simple occurrence. God's first speech, though it may intimidate a human audience, is otherwise received by the angelic listeners:

> *Thus while God spake, ambrosial fragrance filled*
> *All heav'n, and in the blessed Spirits elect*
> *Sense of new joy ineffable diffused.*
> *(III, 135–37)*

The "Sense of new joy" is an anticipation of new knowledge, which is to be revealed by the Son, whose voluntary task it is to interpret the Father's words and act accordingly. The consequences of Milton's concept cannot be confined to the purposes of an embellishment yielding a momentary satisfaction. Besides—to touch on a point we shall need to explore further—Milton is highly conscious of what any authoritative beginning must present. First impressions are important in the rhetoric of art as it imitates human nature, but insofar as art aspires to imitate divine creation, what it presents will also bear the visible signs of the inner principles which form and govern. Milton can make bold and varied uses of the authority of beginnings, and *Paradise Lost* provides him with great opportunities which he does not neglect. What we cannot miss in the above example, but cannot comprehend at once in all its consequences, is that the free perfection of heaven, more authoritative than that of a Golden Age, is a state of perfection in which both choice and trial (even though not "by what is contrary") are at home.[7] The perfection is, furthermore, an evolving one, and the novelty of change is welcomed as the "Sense of new joy ineffable" to which the trial of the Son is about to give permanent expression.

The concept of evolving perfection does not escape Satan's commentary:

> *O earth, how like to heav'n, if not preferred*
> *More justly, seat worthier of gods, as built*
> *With second thoughts, reforming what was old!*
> *For what God after better worse would build?*
> *(IX, 99–102)*

Satan is clearly speaking for himself, translating the philosophical language into his own terms, not without solecism. Upon another occasion, answering Abdiel, he puts together a conservative rejection of the new, an extreme empiricism, and his personal, impromptu theory of self-creation under the auspices of cyclical time:

> *Strange point and new!*
> *Doctrine which we would know whence learnt.*
> *Who saw*
> *When this creation was? Remember'st thou*
> *Thy making, while the Maker gave thee being?*
> *We know no time when we were not as now;*
> *Know none before us, self-begot, self-raised*
> *By our own quick'ning power, when fatal course*
> *Had circled his full orb, the birth mature*
> *Of this our native heav'n, ethereal sons.*
> *(V, 854–63)*

In part Milton can rely on Satan's hodgepodge opportunism and egocentricity to deflect the fragments of truth frequently embedded in his discourse. But we cannot so easily enjoy, or be certain how we are to interpret, a similar strain in the expression of the unfallen Adam. (I shall offer the best interpretation I can manage at this point, but the issue will in some important ways remain alive throughout the poem, and we shall need to regard it from evolving and partly different perspectives.)

In describing the second stage of his creation, after leaving the beautiful world outside to enter "the garden of bliss, thy seat prepared," Adam responds with a "Sense of new joy" and declares "that what I saw / Of earth before scarce pleasant seemed." Not long afterward he tells of his first view of Eve, a narration that is not marked by clear distinction of time or appraisal, and is less a telling than the acting out of a response that seems to overtake and match, like accompanying music, the shape of Eve emerging:

> *Under his forming hands a creature grew,*
> *Man-like, but different sex, so lovely fair*
> *That what seemed fair in all the world seemed now*
> *Mean, or in her summed up, in her contained*
> *And in her looks. . . .*
> *(VIII, 470–74)*

The first celebration of the world outside man is the spontaneous expression of a unique experience: man finds himself alive, mature, just created. Everything he says and does must express the pure truth of an authentic beginning. The problems we shall concentrate on, however, concern the state of waking dream and the implications of Adam's first comparisons. At first, Adam is fully awake though his preceding state was non-existence: "As new-waked from soundest sleep." Then he enters Paradise in a waking dream, having heard God speak, having been led "as in air / Smooth sliding without step." There he makes his comparison unfavorable to the world outside and sees

> *Each tree*
> *Loaden with fairest fruit, that hung to the eye*
> *Tempting, stirred in me sudden appetite*
> *To pluck and eat; whereat I waked, and found*
> *Before mine eyes all real, as the dream*
> *Had lively shadowed.*
> *(VIII, 306–11)*

It is the somnolent state that still chiefly concerns us. After the long dialogue that leads to the creation of Eve, Adam is again reduced to sleep, this time in a more elaborate ritual of preparation. He feels exhausted by the strain of the "celestial colloquy . . . As with an object that excels the sense." Sleep comes instantly, but his imagination remains awake,

> my internal sight, by which
> Abstract as in a trance methought I saw. . . .
> *(VIII, 461–62)*

The simple underlying pattern is this: the first celebration of the first world seen is made when Adam is fully awake; the first comparison, which spontaneously disparages the outside world, and the second comparison, which suggests that the sight of Eve induces a momentary impulse to despise *everything* thus far seen, are both made by Adam in a state of waking dream.

How are we to interpret the implications of comparisons that suggest disparagement, a kind of turning away, perhaps rejection? Though they are couched in carefully tentative language, and are further protected by the traditions of making allowances for the hyperboles and transiencies in the groping candor of precipitate speech, Adam's comparisons are ominous—even if we restrain the tendency to impose our foreknowledge of Adam's later act of decisive rejection. The right order of ascending value in the poem includes the lower in the higher, and the continuity is unbroken except by the rejection of elements that are clearly adverse to life and its higher purposes.[8] God creating from the material of chaos first purges "The black tartareous cold infernal dregs." The Satanic host, expelled from heaven, still is (for the poem) too necessary a bad example to lose all connections with the right order at once. Sin and Death are assigned a fixed function, "to lick up the draff and filth" of sin until the second coming of Christ. But these examples cannot in any coherent way refer to Adam's verbal actions, which seem to have no substantial analogues in the poem. One may perhaps add the strange remark that Adam lets slip when he thanks God for the fairest "Of all thy gifts, nor enviest." This is the Adam of awkward joy, stumbling on a concept not unfamiliar to primitive religious thought, or to a line of anxiety Satan will try to stimulate in Eve. But the remark here is isolated and seems almost an accident, until its potentiality comes alive at the fall. Or one may perhaps feel some remote resemblance between Adam's impulse to disparage lesser joy and Satan's loss of all pleasure but the relief of destruction. Again, the most we could claim with assurance is that these hints of potentiality are ominous but are too fleeting to be taken as evidence.

Adam's first comparison, "Scarce pleasant seemed," is a qualified hyperbole, not unfamiliar in speakers aware that their language is inexact and influenced by the surprise of a new experience not yet understood. It is a wrong imagination, but in the moral rules of freedom to which the poem is committed, there is no blame attached to a random thought which is not approved by being acted upon. The hyperbole produced by the first sight of Eve is more radical: in comparison with her the beauty of everything else now seemed "Mean." But a censoring awareness in Adam at once begins to revise his first expression. He adds: "or in her summed up, in her contained." This is to anticipate, in the first example of love at first sight, the traditional exaggerations of love, by which the beloved becomes a garden in herself. Eve presents her own summing-up, and affirms the correct order of ascending value which includes the lower in the higher, when she acknowledges

> *How beauty is excelled by manly grace*
> *And wisdom, which alone is truly fair.*
> *(IV, 490–91)*

Even Satan is made to testify, though under special stress, to the rightness of the ascending order:

> *Much he the place admired, the person more.*
> *As one who long in populous city pent . . .*
> *If chance with nymph-like step fair virgin pass,*
> *What pleasing seemed, for her now pleases more,*
> *She most, and in her looks sums all delight.*
> *(IX, 444–54)*

Nevertheless, the impulse to reject implied by Adam's negative summation, "Mean," remains troubling. The expression is stronger, more deeply committed, than "Scarce pleasant seemed." It is less fleeting, less isolated; for the instant revision that offers another interpretation, a better one, emphasizes by acknowledgement the questionable first response. We are witnessing with Adam an authentic beginning, a first impression in which governing principles inhere.

They need not be obvious (and we have not yet touched them), but the moment is a serious one and the poet should not indulge in whimsical distractions of the decorative or the adventitious. Are we being prompted to observe in human nature a tendency to reject which is at odds with the purposes of divine creation? If so, then Milton is allowing some slackness to intrude into his austere concepts of justice and freedom, and we must hasten to some Empsonian forms of reasoning. But perhaps not yet.

Implied in Adam's behavior is an aspiring restlessness of heart which is not at odds with divine purpose. In his great soliloquy upon first awakening into life he responds to the beauty of the world about him, but as part of the process of reasoning out the existence of a Maker whom he wishes to know and adore. There is no implied rejection, but there is a marked advance to a higher stage. Adam's own existence is not completed when he is transferred to Paradise; he must there reason out the need for Eve, which God's prescience approves and grants. When Adam fixes his heart on Eve, the sense of fulfillment is natural and certainly not without sanction. On the one hand, by way of sympathetic extenuation, we may observe the background of that long dialogue with God, and Adam's eager eloquence against solitude as a proper human state, and observe the sense of exhaustion. All of these may be thought to contribute, in a natural way, to a momentary over-reaction, though Milton is not the kind of writer to found ultimate justifications on the impulses of a natural way. Adam's eagerness, and the argument against solitude, are, to be sure, accepted by God—not without some benevolent amusement at the rational happiness proposed by the choice of "associates" and at His creature's resolution to enjoy "No pleasure, though in pleasure, solitary." This last expression, of God's approving humor, does not leave exposed to the onus of possible willfulness what would otherwise seem to be an expression corroborating Adam's first despising of the world apart from Eve:

> *She disappeared, and left me dark; I waked*
> *To find her, or for ever to deplore*
> *Her loss, and other pleasures all abjure.*
> *(VIII, 478–80)*

He will arrive at the state where not to join Eve in disobedience is to risk living "again in these wild woods forlorn."

That attitude and the accompanying decision will then "approve" whatever evil was in the first random thought implying rejection. But Milton cannot intend the first response to foreshadow in any binding way the later response. His story, if he is in control of it, precludes a standard cause-and-effect passage from innocence to sin.

On the other hand, Adam's first response *should* trouble us, and not less because the rules of the story forbid a deterministic interpretation and forbid attributing what is wrong in Adam's imagination to his Maker or his making. To prevent our questioning, Milton might have stabilized Adam's initial excitement over Eve by having him correct his first statement more thoroughly—for instance, making it clear that she sums up the beauty of the world and leads toward the higher beauty, of which she is an acknowledged gift. Even Satan, though not a lover, can be moved by the beauty of "divine resemblance." No one ought to regret Milton's preferring to suppress that clarification. We must instead observe that he does suppress it, and ask ourselves why. He can be emphatic enough when he wants to read out the moral directions, but remarkably reticent when he wants the reader to exercise his own freedom of choice. We are being shown an initial potentiality that we recognize as humanly dangerous, but we are denied our usual practice of establishing motive and relying on the usual guides of narrative continuity. Instead, we see a troubling response at a significant moment and cannot place what we see into a regular chain of evidence.

To these questions that we have been exploring I propose a simple answer that does not, I believe, render useless our trying to understand the problems Milton has released. From the first stage of his creation, through the birth of Eve, Adam has been "tried" by God: "Thus far to try thee, Adam, I was pleased." The animals which Adam has "rightly named" were "for trial only brought," to test Adam's knowledge and judgment both of the beasts and of himself. And God is satisfied that Adam has expressed His image, "the spirit within thee free." (Soon Adam will invent his own occasion for trial, with Raphael as a less-approving witness.) These trials are all preliminary ones, and Adam emerges innocent (we have God's word), but the conditions of his existence have shaded in, as it were, some suggestions of development in spite of the formal obstacles which prevent psychological and narrative progress.

The materials of adversity are limited in the garden, as in heaven, but Milton can turn the materials of prosperity to good use. There is a line of progression from Adam's first awakening which leads to the sense of fulfillment at the creation of Eve, which brings his "story to the sum of earthly bliss." Any new joy potentially on the divine schedule will now require mastering the sphere of activity "assigned," "Reaping immortal fruits of . . . Uninterrupted joy, unrivaled love" while retaining—which means giving and receiving—

> *Unalterably firm his love entire*
> *Whose progeny you are.*
>
> *(V, 502–03)*

Without a qualitative change of state, further joy is impossible; human nature is declared to be "incapable of more." Quantitative increase will be a delusion available on the Satanic schedule. Yet "Uninterrupted joy," like managing the affairs of daily life, contains the matter of trial, the potentiality of both good and ill. From this point of view the impulse to despise lesser joy at the sight of a greater one is a preliminary temptation for Adam, one that creates a scope of mental action within the limited boundaries of innocence. That action has the further purpose of validating the effective presence of freedom, which authorizes the random thoughts that will be dangerous only if they are followed through. Adam is living more dangerously than the ordinary musings on Paradise would prepare one to expect, but his capacity for choice remains unimpaired by the experience we have witnessed.

By assigning Adam's ambiguous responses to the state of waking dream, Milton, whatever else he intends, is also emphasizing the noncommittal status of the suggestions that emerge. They are carefully set spart and marked off at one remove. God presides over the dream state, but by the strict rules of freedom whatever foreknowledge is involved should neither motivate nor influence the event. Thus Adam, before he wakes in Paradise, fastens his sight on the fruit of various trees; the effect, "Tempting, stirred in me sudden appetite / To pluck and eat." The moment of course has its ominous aspect but is also perfectly natural and morally neutral.[9] When he wakes from his second dream state to find Eve gone, he determines

> *To find her, or for ever to deplore*
> *Her loss, and other pleasures all abjure.*
> *(VIII, 479–80)*

Though foreknowledge may see ominousness in his attitude,
what he says is not out of keeping with the dialogue that led
to her creation. The abjuring of pleasure under the shock of a
sudden loss is not quite the same as disparaging lesser joy at
the sight of a greater. Though abjuring may be a small first
step in the direction of Satan's ultimate state of finding relief
only in destruction, it is at most a small step of alienation, a
trial of human love and not yet a moral crisis. Satan is an
extreme case, far advanced and beyond the point of recovery.
Adam is in love, at first sight, a condition in which some
bewilderment may be expected and forgiven by God as well as
man. When Adam, "out of hope," finally does rediscover Eve,
the awakened language of love is unimpeachable:

> *Such as I saw her in my dream, adorned*
> *With what all earth or heaven could bestow*
> *To make her amiable. On she came,*
> *Led by her heav'nly Maker, though unseen,*
> *And guided by his voice, nor uninformed*
> *Of nuptial sanctity and marriage rites.*
> *Grace was in all her steps, heav'n in her eye.*
> *In every gesture dignity and love.*
> *(VIII, 482–89)*

She does sum up all the world's beauty. Yet the attributions
borrowed from thoughts of heaven, though they do not trouble, naturally and unobtrusively contain the matter of trial,
however muted.

If the main lines of the preceding discussion seem worth
entertaining, we have a basis for further observations and
questions. To look back briefly: Milton can write about the
first Paradise without any fixed sense of returning to the ultimate model of human life, where desire is at rest in its
source, the end in the beginning. For Milton the experience is
the foundation of a story which cannot achieve the right dignity and scope without commensurate length. Nor is he
cramped and confined because his subject is the "first disobedience," the failure of Paradise. No one has written as
well and as fully on Paradise, on the beauty of the first world,

and on God's creative love. These are the grounds, necessary for a long story that will not reach its tragic moment of reversal until Adam decides to be ruined, not until seven-tenths of the poem has unfolded.

The narrative must be conducted under certain uncompromising rules and circumstances. The theme of human failure is announced in the first words of the poem, and the exacting conditions of freedom are promulgated from the throne of God. Though the outcome is to be expected, it cannot be produced by anything mindless, like historical accident, something imposed on the actors from without, a surprise they do not deserve. Yet any strain of consecutive inclination that may weaken the capacity of the hero to stand on "even ground" until the decisive moment will weaken the demonstration of human freedom and divine justice. To tell the whole story and tell it rightly, Milton's imagination must work both backward and forward, and must draw on the deep conviction that trial is the will of a benevolent deity presiding over a universe that evolves toward ultimate good.

These conditions, successfully met, may be illustrated by God's praise of the Son's voluntary act of immortal love for mortal men, by which he has "been found / By merit more than birthright Son of God." The absoluteness of the source, the divine "birthright," has been demonstrated to be what it is, which trial cannot imaginably diminish or augment. The "more" has to be taken as God's language thoughtfully accommodated to angelic (and human) understanding, taken as an instructive expression of His pleasure at seeing the laws of freedom work in accordance with His will. At the same time the "Sense of new joy" is validated by an exemplary action.

Adam's early trials have demonstrated a lesser but still satisfactory correspondence between "merit" and "birthright." Then, at the noon of his prosperity, "incapable of more" earthy bliss, he must prove the firmness of his "love entire.'" His love for Eve is part of his birthright, and her creation is placed by God in a context of trial resembling the Son's free expression of divine will. If the governing laws hold true Adam's "love entire" must include, but cannot be summed up by, his love for Eve. On the other hand, the love due God does not authorize unfavorable comparisons, by which, for instance, human love might seem "scarce pleasant" or "mean."

II.

Truth, Novelty, and Choice

Though true beginnings of "birthright" are proved by free trials of "merit," a system of testing, constantly and prominently applied, might prove heavy freight to a poem that aspires to soar adventurously. Much of the testing is therefore subtle and fine, moving under the surface toward the points of crisis. In addition, for the first two books Milton makes it easy for his readers, treating them like those fit students in his idea of an academy who pick up the right preliminary knowledge while thoroughly enjoying themselves. By the time we emerge from hell and the imaginative opportunities which the author fully exploits, we have been well exercised and trained for more serious adventure.

There is another way in which Milton counterbalances the prominent emphasis on trial. He brings into his poem the solid weight of the inherited truths of wisdom, the authoritative knowledge of things divine and human drawn from Scripture and from every branch of human discourse. Yet some of these materials deliberately reinforce, even as texture, the constant presence of trial, for truths may be misplaced, or wrongly timed, or otherwise distorted in context. But then some truths, secular as well as sacred in derivation, are not questioned and tested as others are. They are *demonstrative* in the older technical sense of the word, truths which need only to shown properly. Like pre-existent principles they can be discovered, elaborately proved, or simply accepted. They are certain and, once they are seen, self-evident. Apparent exceptions prove some hidden wrongness in the thinker, actor, or observer. Such truths are for the poet—if we make due allowances—not wholly unlike a divine fact of spirituality asserted by God:

> *Some I have chosen of peculiar grace*
> *Elect above the rest; so is my will.*
> *(III, 183–84)*

If such truths are accepted we understand circumstances and connections; if not, like the philosophical angels of hell, or Adam in sustained contemplation after the fall, we wander in mazes.

In spite of the Christian poet's bardic humility, and his acknowledged dependence on the heavenly Muse for ventures into darkness and light, and into the lesser, but more personal difficulties of the "narrower bound" on earth, these expressions of personal modesty and limitation do not impede his access to the most remote and authoritative truths:

> *And chiefly thou, O Spirit, that dost prefer*
> *Before all temples th' upright heart and pure,*
> *Instruct me, for thou know'st; thou from the first*
> *Wast present.*
> *(I, 17–20)*

Such truths, though clearly dependent upon the poet's long pondering over "those written records pure, / Though not but by the Spirit understood," require further help commensurate with the goals of the epic enterprise. These truths are fundamental to the assertion of Providence and to the manifestation of justice in "the ways of God to men."

We may perhaps identify the poet's long and deliberate preparation with a preliminary trial of merit. But it is difficult to draw with assurance a line between his birthright and merit—given what we know of Milton's own serious views of his early studies and of his mature career as champion of civil, religious, and domestic liberty. In a life consciously devoted to learning, knowing, and striving to translate knowledge into intellectual action leading to public good, the expressions of desire and ability in the proofs of action do not easily lend themselves to categorical separation, but may seem rather to be all of a piece, composite, proved gifts. Even when reluctant, Old Testament prophets illustrate the problems introduced when inspired vocation becomes identical with birthright. God surely had the prophets in mind, as did Milton, who might also hope the divine assertion would reach his own case when he had God announce:

Some I have chosen of peculiar grace
Elect above the rest; so is my will.

If the poet indeed possesses an "upright heart and pure," and is truly inspired, we shall find uncommon difficulties in attempting to distinguish between the endowment of birthright and the more-or-less of the proof of merit. As for the truths themselves, in a discourse on literature we may well exceed our credentials even in the limited task of judging the poet's effective possession and expression of truths.

To venture an illustrative comparison with obvious reservations: the trial of the poet is not wholly unlike the trial of the Son in Book III. The poet's choice of basic truths ought to accord with what good men believe to be the will of God. Asserting "Eternal Providence" will require demonstrations that convince, but without the apparatus of formal argument and trial indispensable to the proof of lesser matters. On the other hand, to "justify the ways of God to men" is less a demonstration than an argument which will depend upon dialectical probability and trial. Milton's argument, to get ahead of our own, is one that aspires to convince by means of a story, a fable, which includes and tests all the suasive human materials of sophistic, rhetoric, and dialectic, and strives to bring the fabulous and the demonstrative into as complete a union as possible.

To offer another illustrative comparison: the trial of the poet is not unlike the trial of Adam in the dialogue with God that leads to the creation of Eve. Here the asserting of Providence is—as it were—subordinated to story and the rules of dialogue, which arrive at truth by an open, examinable process of probability. In the process God's ways and Adam's ways are "justified." In the largest sense the poet's trial is continuous throughout the poem; the evidence ranges from the minutiae of consonants and syllables to the choices of greatest consequence to his design, which test the truth of his inspiration and the merit of his action.

Though Milton is both critical and committed in his handling of inherited truths, he is also encyclopedic. Few topics from the then-known history of religious and secular thought are not represented in his epic. It is perhaps enough to assert these matters in general and to rely on the evidence of printed scholarship. If Milton's essential ideas are few, he may be said to reflect the history of thought in this respect. On the other hand, his secondary ideas are numerous and are drawn from a vast variety of sources. They appear in explicit or implicit form, as direct statement or digest or glancing allusion, as the thread which guides the sense of a passage, as a synoptic view which indicates the good or bad or doubtful drift of meaning, as the reflecting surfaces that figures of speech illuminate and are illuminated by. The general effect is massive, but the single effects are subtle, varied in kind and in degree of prominence. From one point of view the weight and scope of articulated truths may seem to stabilize the movements toward change which are announced from the beginning and which impend throughout. But there are tensions, too, as the truths are tested, as God's ways are justified in linked argument, and as the story strives to fulfill its ordinary and extraordinary functions.

One of the great opportunities of the story is that it antedates all other stories, and therefore Milton's readers will find themselves often recognizing thoughts in a novel form, before they become original familiar quotations. Within the controlling perspective of time, not seldom the myth alluded to is still to be invented. (Or if the perspective yields the acknowledged existence of the myth, its cognitive and emotional value may be borrowed powerfully under a mild disclaimer—most notably in "Not that fair field / Of Enna.") Famous passages of literature, imitated or transformed or rewritten with the cool intention of surpassing them, are not yet famous for they have not yet been composed. They may even be criticized in the formula of a scholarly theologian reproving the misguided interpretation of a predecessor, *errat*, but Milton's dismissal can be laid down as if in advance, telling the real story which will be travestied in ancient Greece while—the world being what it is—still enjoying currency: "thus they relate / Erring."[1] The reader is made to adjust continually to shifts in the perspective of time and distance.

The surprises of time include the recognition of subsequent truths or events which derive from, or are brought into novel connections with, a poetic retelling of the oldest account of the oldest events in human history and prehistory. The effects are so striking and varied that their employment is not adequately described as a literary device, nor perhaps as an established method or strategy, and one would like to stop short of assigning the effects to the mysterious compass of a poetic vision. Intricacies which are characterized by precision, which are put together so that they can be inspected but neither unraveled completely nor summed up and translated into a single applicable meaning, suggest both calculation on the part of the author and a dimension of movement that cannot be conceived in advance.

At the level of preconception, at least, the analytical reader has available to him the same instruments of thought as the author, and the two of them may possibly meet on the same grounds of departure. At the level of movement, however, the reader cannot imagine the poet's point of departure, or what occurs in his mind before or while the words come. Once the words have been written, fixed in place, and the concentrated intensity of composition has moved on, the poet and the reader both share certain limitations differing but in degree. The poet turning back is himself then a reader, and even to revise he must forget some of the complexity of his initial attention in composing. Those aspects of meaning which are generated by and depend upon the relations of words to each other in movement escape analytical thought, which must separate, arrest, and then recompose, employing its own instruments of thought. The reader will find that he cannot immobilize movement without some distortion or loss of meaning, which he cannot avoid in advance or wholly correct by any later substitution.

One may well believe that Milton sought many effects deliberately but in the process of composition also enjoyed the great artistic privilege of being sought. He seems able to leave himself open to free imaginings that appear to flow in spontaneous response to the development of an immediate situation, while in retrospect what he has written proves to be precise, a flourish with a touch so exact and rich in consequences that to propose change or omission would seem like an act of violence.

If one believes that many of the most difficult things cannot be done at all unless easily, one will not be inclined to challenge the substance of Milton's debt to the Muse:

> *my celestial patroness, who deigns*
> *Her nightly visitations unimplored,*
> *And dictates to me slumb'ring, or inspires*
> *Easy my unpremeditated verse.*
> *(IX, 21–24)*

Still, one cannot assign all the evidence of poetic premeditation and choice to the Muse, though heavenly, and identified—in a circumspect verbal reservation by a master of words—with "The meaning, not the name." In the poem he allows no separation between the name and the meaning of freedom, except for the purposes of displaying perversity. Whatever is attributable to the Muse, Milton nowhere gives hard evidence of wishing to reduce his own proper responsibility for his words and the choices they involve. The general issue is not one that can be resolved by critical assertion. Milton was, it should not be difficult to believe, supported by inspiration; he also learned to think of his poetic materials in ways not visible to us, but so *freely* that much we admire indeed seems "easy," or even "unpremeditated."

I intend to use the word "novelty" in what seems a proper, neutral way; the word has not, like "innovation," been tainted by a flux of sentimental applause. What we find in Milton for the most part is "The meaning, not the name," but the meaning is frequent and worth trying to understand. The harshest use of the name itself occurs in Adam's rejection of Eve's efforts to console him:

> *O why did God,*
> *Creator wise, that peopled highest heav'n*
> *With Spirits masculine, create at last*
> *This novelty on earth, this fair defect*
> *Of Nature, and not fill the world at once*
> *With men as angels without feminine,*
> *Or find some other way to generate*
> *Mankind? This mischief had not then befall'n.*
> *(X, 888–95)*

When Adam concludes this angry speech some twenty lines later, having relieved himself by prophesying on the calamitous predicaments of love, Eve will move him to another "novelty on earth," the first example of one human creature forgiving another. Underneath the single-minded clamor of Adam's expression there are intimations not only that his feelings are wrong but that they sense they are wrong. Because Milton accepts as true the traditions of psychological thought, extended, refined, and never seriously challenged for two thousand years, he is master of the principle most fully displayed in the speech of Satan, that the language of disturbed feelings is governed by a secret code which signals, through distress, the obscure movements of reason and choice. In Adam's speech Milton applies the principle with a

heavy hand and a witty humorlessness, for Adam is commit-
ting a kind of perjury and betrayal of an earlier state of feelings
too deep and authoritative to be revised by the glib eloquence
of anger. Only on second thought, by virtue of Satanic lapses
and omissions, does Eve become a novelty in a hateful sense
that exposes coarse habits of (future) human thought which
react with blind fear and hatred toward the new or the other,
and with partly blind cunning project all blame against whatever is not clearly to one's present and long-range advantage.

Though the passage has a depressing history as a prized text
for proving Milton's terrible misogyny, in the present climate
of opinion informed readers will recognize that the speech is
dramatic, and that the author's immediate purpose is to
exhibit "a fierce reflux" redounding. Nor is the author com-
mitting himself to the reliable accuracy of the speech as it
prophesies on the calamities of love and on the revelations of
female character. As for the author's possible involvement in
the unacknowledged aim of some personal expression, to
interpret the passage so, one must regard Milton as either
naive or blinded by the grip of his feelings—to unpack his
own heart with the angry words of a self-deceiving partisan
backing away from his recent recognition that evasions and
reasonings are vain, but that "all the blame lights due" on
himself alone.

At the other extreme we have a novelty not called so, Milton's invention of the dialogue in heaven, that primary model
of freedom and much else, an episode which proves the rightness of the angelic anticipation of "new joy" and releases the
synoptic view of Providence rising to the apocalyptic vision
when "God shall be all in all." The vision of the end of things,
the final episode, as it were, that punctuates eternity, cannot
be thought novel in any ordinary sense. The scriptural basis
in the Book of Revelation provides one of the most widely
shared nightmares of western religious thought, the lurid
symbolism repeatedly interpreted and charted, fixed in
schemes by which one could establish bearings that claimed
to locate the position of the ever-perilous present in relation
to the grip of that last unfolding. Though there was no
unanimity on the meaning of details, and no authoritative
code that could translate the message to everyone's satisfaction, the general sense was clear enough to achieve, with
some of the more unnerving symbolism, a pervasive domestic familiarity.

Milton's treatment is novel in a double sense. The episode is one that, since it has haunted thought in strange and particular ways, can never be produced without a kind of perverse novelty, the excitement aroused by an impending cosmic threat-and-promise, an old dream scanned anew. The episode is the largest frame of Milton's story, an assertion of Providence which closes the full circle and encompasses everything. But Milton's treatment is novel in the sense that it is remarkably simple and matter-of-fact, sparing in detail and stimulation, a prophecy, not a nightmare renewed and acting out its imagined arrival. The vision of the end is, on balance, mostly one of promise; as the largest frame it is firmly in place but in a special place. Perhaps at that furthest verge of time and the moral universe one cannot discriminate between the justification of God's ways and the assertion of Providence. Milton would seem to intend no room for difference at that coalescing point. But the special place of the largest frame is clear as well as firm: its place is that of benevolent detachment. Grander in sweep and compass than the separate actions and periods of foreknowledge, and not ever-present as an immediate shadow without impulse—for reasons as immutable as those which order God's foreknowledge, the encompassing vision also refrains from influencing events, from imposing its existence upon the freedom of intermediate action.

In between the extremes represented by Adam's "This novelty on earth" and God's quiet version of the encompassing vision, Milton is master of a full range of novelty. His standards were, of course, those of an enlightened humanist for whom originality could not be either guiding principle or conscious goal. He would have scorned the thought of solving the problems of his accepted materials by imposing utterly new and therefore personal interpretations, in order to write the first "witty" epic. In *Paradise Lost* his mind is not less but more bold than in the prose that champions revolution, and part of the reason is that he must handle all of the tenacious arguments himself, and without the narrowing stimulation that external opponents can be expected to produce. The poet must consider more deeply the consequences and the placing of the new among the old, and therefore in the poem Milton is also—perhaps to a surprising extent—conservative. He satisfies all of the reader's sure knowledge of events, circumstances and outcome. Besides, where knowledge is not

established by Scripture or the traditions of human agreement, if expectations nevertheless exist and are firm and
deep, Milton carefully subordinates the appearances of originality. His tact in these uncharted areas displays a knowledge
of the human heart which, however surpassed by the bulk of
his other learning, is essential to his poetic task. As a means
of understanding his own sense of his work and its problems,
it is instructive to observe where and how he feels free to
indulge and where to curb his fancy. Whole books of the
poem, as the adventures of hell and chaos or the war in
heaven, clearly invite the novel on a large scale. Elsewhere
the novelty seems almost subliminal, as in the example discussed in the last chapter, Adam's impulse to reject suggested
by the comparisons of his waking dreams.

We are on solid ground when we observe the deliberate
novelties Milton intersperses among the ranked truths of
traditional thought. Like the truths themselves, the novelties
differ in kind and in the weight of significance they bring to
the poem. Some are presented as the obvious or subtle material of trial, while some reflect the order of evolving Providence. Others may be associated with the narrative challenge, and the trial of the poet himself, in telling the oldest
story as if for the first time—transforming well-worn familiarity into fresh immediacy, returning simple events to their
moment of occurrence, freed from the encumbering bulk of
industrious commentary, so that the events can be felt as
story, simple, sensuous, passionate, as "unattempted yet."

The narrative challenge, even in the matter of novelty, is by
no means limited to the purposes enumerated above. One
could perhaps classify the uses and kinds of novelty Milton
employs, and there are enough of them for a monograph on
his art of novelty. His main preference, as one might anticipate, seems to be for multiple effects. For any emphatic
novelty will suggest the possible presence of choice and trial,
and may produce reverberations among the surrounding inherited truths, and will always strike a kind of chronological
chord expressing the surprises of time. This last may *declare*,
answering a question, whether asked or not (like the prominence, praise, and dignity of human work in the Garden), or
may produce the sense of a question and the esthetic expectation of an answer, because of some dissonance or suggested
tension in the sounding of past-present-future.

If one were attempting a classification, one should perhaps

need to consider the uses of novelty as part of the rhetoric of surprise, which is as basic and constant in Milton's art as the characteristically suspended syntax, the unpredictable turns of phrase, the commanding power and grace of rhythms moving over uneven contours we do not anticipate. It pleases him to bring an element of surprise into the expected, even into the inevitable. To recognize novelty, which seldom escapes notice and often gives the impression of having emerged suddenly, is to feel surprise, whatever else the experience may contain.

In order to take up some of these matters together—the varied functions of novelty in relation to traditional thought and the trial of choice—let us consider two sections of the poem which present novelty in widely different ways and for different purposes. The second example will be Adam's account of the discovery of passion. The first is that splendid extravagance which seems to be complete novelty, the building of Pandemonium in its larger context of surprises.

The context is, of course, a major accomplishment in itself, and a striking example of Milton's particular interest in the way poems begin as well as end. One advantage of Milton's underworld is that he does not need to respect or actively counter the traditions attached to the Christian hell, but can indulge in sheer virtuosity of imaginative play. From the point of view of the poem, Virgil did take a long and useful glimpse into the underworld, but much later; most of Dante's great enterprise does not have to be taken into account. The hell of Milton's fable is populated only by fallen angels and not yet by men. The displays are based upon a conception of decaying grandeur—connected by varied reference to the good and evil of the future world, and reflecting, not a single and fixed stage of perversion from original truth, but a dynamic perversion capable of suggesting present and future development. When we emerge from hell, Milton will have already accomplished an important part of his task of presenting unfallen truth—by the reader's long exposure to the "darkness visible" of truth deteriorating. The subsequent history of Satan will review, consolidate, and extend the implications, in order to create a fully developed background against which the small movements permissible in the presentation of Adam and Eve can be magnified.

One of the most useful comments on the first two books is Milton's brief definition of greatness: "He alone is to be

called great who either performs or teaches or worthily records great things."[2] Milton does not say, but he clearly demonstrates by his own practice, that the power to describe false
greatness with suitable dignity may be inferred from his
definition. Though we are suddenly plunged into the amazing
complexities which play heroic games with heroics, the skill
which so displays itself nevertheless maintains a sense of
delicately balanced control and separation. Ironic reference
and comparison punctuate and guide, so that we may enjoy
the imaginative excursions even while we question them for
their real meaning or suspend judgment confidently expecting meanings to emerge. Behind the deliberate excesses are
the monuments of authentic epic grandeur, heightened and
applied in ways that expose what is being discountenanced
while not undermining the sources and possibilities of true
grandeur. The style mocks and parodies, not by the easy
techniques of burlesque, by simply over-expanding the pos-
tures, activities, and speeches of the false, but by the most
difficult way, by a rational laughter that makes the symbols
of evil include what evil has borrowed from the origins and
traditions of heroic dignity.

The poet may stand apart, and when we think of the problem we may find it most difficult to locate him in what is
being said, but we can usually locate ourselves in the double
vision to which the symbols of evil are subjected. The general
point is one we shall return to, but the essential point is that
underneath Milton's complex games is an unwavering belief
in true greatness and its origin in radical simplicity. Much of
the force which guides his presentation of hell derives from a
certainty that the false is a wrong-minded imitation of the
true. Perhaps the plainest example is the response of the
fallen angels to their simple longing for the light of heaven—
the invention of interior lighting:

> *from the arched roof*
> *Pendent by subtle magic many a row*
> *Of starry lamps and blazing cressets fed*
> *With naphtha and asphaltus yielded light*
> *As from a sky.*
>
> (I, 726–30)

That the exemplary punishment of an irreversible falling
away from truth is a perverted longing for truth, provides him
with a classic subject for laughter. Milton's comic vein, to

state the obvious, has little sympathy with the common di-
lemmas of human bumbling; his laughter almost always has
an edge. But the grandeur of his imagination has its own kind
of generosity which sponsors an appropriate laughter. Even in
hell the purpose of laughter may be subordinated to larger
considerations, and artistic generosity in writing of hell cannot be expressed without the taking of risks, one of which
may be the writer's exposing his own efforts to laughter.

The effect of music, for instance, in that spectacular, moving parade of the fallen angels, takes place in a context governed by a comic perspective, our practical knowledge of
parades as a standard ritual for raising general morale. But the
effect of music upon "troubled thoughts" in "mortal or immortal minds," while not blurring the immediate comic
perspective, does extend both the power of music and the
power of sympathy. The difference between the fallen angels
"raised / To highth of noblest temper," though sustained in
illusion, and Adam and Eve departing from Paradise is the
difference between the support of eternal Providence and a
moment of art. The scenes are memorable, however, not only
because the difference is absolute, but because the pathos is
similar. One may say the same of those divisions between
judgment and feeling, first exercised in hell, as preparation for
the sustained discipline we shall need in attending to the
story of Adam and Eve. Or to take another example, a simpler
one, but nevertheless involving some risks on the part of the
author: Milton has been patronized for his extravagant description of Satan's "eyes / That sparkling blazed." Milton's
more hazardous incongruity seems to pass unchallenged,
that of amplifying Satan's orations to the highest pitch of
public style, as if for the millions, while directed only to "his
nearest mate," Beelzebub, while both of them are lying prone
and the orator has been developing all that volume with only
his head "uplift above the waves."

The double vision developed in hell, though it involves a
kind of silent laughter, chiefly serves a larger purpose of training the reader's imagination, patience, and judgment, teaching him how to see the small in the apparently great; the
reverse of that proposition will come later as a more difficult
lesson. Hence the many surprises that bring imaginative
awareness to bear upon actions involving mass and time.
That grimly sustained travesty of the epic catalogue, the
roll-call of heathen gods-to-be, provides an almost-unrelieved

counterbalance to the frequent and briefer imaginative episodes which are balanced within themselves. For instance, we see Satan's massive shield through the glass of Galileo's telescope trained on the moon; human responses to size, distance, and time are stimulated and suspended in the reflected consciousness of privilege and magnified viewing, and in the imaginative movements between there and here, then and now. The sense of being stimulated and suspended is also on Milton's curriculum for improving the fitness of the reader. A simpler example, less densely ordered, and with more extravagant delight in the pleasures of virtuosity, plays with the interchangeability of size, remoteness, and function:

> *His spear, to equal which the tallest pine*
> *Hewn on Norwegian hills, to be the mast*
> *Of some great ammiral, were but a wand,*
> *He walked with to support uneasy steps. . . .*
> *(I, 292–95)*

Another kind of order follows at once, this time imposed with a display of imaginative arbitrariness not wholly unlike a divine "so is my will," permitting no room for demurral in the press of stimulated interest. We witness a sequence of metamorphoses which turns the fallen angels into "autumnal leaves" or "scattered sedge" on the Red Sea, where once the army pursuing the chosen people was turned into "floating carcasses / And broken chariot wheels," into which by suggested resemblance the fallen angels are turned again:

> *so thick bestrown,*
> *Abject and lost lay these, covering the flood,*
> *Under amazement of their hideous change.*
> *(I, 311–13)*

The final change is presented as an image of mass to the eye, discriminated chiefly by the points of comparison selected and named for the mind. Left open is the bridge of "perfidious hatred" between the two armies and their intended victims, past and future. We are stimulated by the imaginative power, by its capacity to move where it wants and to fill our minds with an unexpected wealth of exactly drawn details, while suspending us in what is not said, in the reservations chosen as deliberately as the pointed comparisons. For the fallen angels have a history of pursuit and destruction in heaven, and a history on earth about to be sketched in the epic roll-call. Left open for the reader to experience on his own is his relationship to the viewers in the central action, which is composed like a painting, an action complete and balanced within itself and seen from a deliberate perspective:

> the Red Sea coast, whose waves o'erthrew
> Busiris and his Memphian chivalry,
> While with perfidious hatred they pursued
> The sojourners of Goshen, who beheld
> From the safe shore their floating carcasses
> And broken chariot wheels . . . .
>
> (I, 306–11)

Our response resembles, I believe, that pattern of being stimulated and suspended which is part of the double vision of hell and may be thought a discipline preparing us for the story of Adam and Eve. As the preceding sentence testifies, one may feel stimulated to search for a larger meaning, and may feel the esthetic expectation of an *answer* because the tensions produced by the passage feel like a *question* in the kind of discourse which art conducts. One may also wonder, in a varied form of suspense, at the expectation that there should be some translatable meaning in Milton's display itself—in such masterful overabundance relishing its power to say far more than expected and to say it irresistibly, giving potential excess the outlines and inner structure of hard precision, saying more than one would have thought possible, and satisfying while still arousing the sense of what is not said.

In the long epic roll-call Milton emphasizes the threatening *otherness* of the fallen angels, and he strengthens this pattern by the many brief references which point to the same end, as in parts of the passage we have been considering. At the same time he fascinates and draws us closer in the pleasure of our imaginative privilege of watching "From the safe shore." That privilege may grant safety and separation, but it may also draw us into the disturbed pleasure of discovering *sameness*—as in the sympathetic power of music to affect "mortal or immortal minds." Milton keeps up a steady emphasis on the similarity, stretching thin but not broken, between good and fallen good. The doctrine is of course orthodox—the concept of good as the one governing principle and of evil as a self-diminishing reaction, with all the symptoms, diagnoses, and prognoses fully worked out and systematized—but the benefits to the poetry are often surprising. A late example is that of Satan about to encounter Eve, which gets its special effect from a witty literal application of traditional thought. When Satan for a moment loses the perverse energy of evil rebounding from good, his relapse leaves him good, without the intelligence and will to act, and so "stupidly good." But Satan is also allowed to enunciate from his own point of view, though perverse, one of the larger truths of the poem, the basis of moral conflict authorized by Providence:

> *If then his providence*
> *Out of our evil seek to bring forth good,*
> *Our labor must be to pervert that end,*
> *And out of good still to find means of evil;*
> *Which ofttimes may succeed, so as perhaps*
> *Shall grieve him, if I fail not, and disturb*
> *His inmost counsels from their destined aim.*
> *(I, 162–68)*

This is an assertion of Providence which Satan can tamper with but not "disturb," though he is given the bold privilege of laying down the issue in his own words and early. That he understands the issue at all is a confirmation of truth-at-the-source, which he is free to oppose or try to pervert, but he cannot destroy the evidence of his knowledge or escape from its effects upon him. The principle involved is one we shall see operating in the interior expression of the soliloquies. It is a principle that will affect Adam's actions and it is accepted by the poet himself in his telling of the story.

Let us now turn to the novelty of the building of Pandemonium, a great *tour de force* which repeats, varies, extends, and—I should like to argue—brings into final focus the context of surprises developed throughout the first book. The narrative action is modest enough—a description of the building, with illustrative references, and an account of the arrangements for accommodating audience and participants. Upon this action Milton constructs an episode exceeded in length only by the epic roll-call, the length of which was determined for reasons other than the nature of the material. At least, Milton could plainly have made the catalogue longer or shorter, with little internal difference in the writing of the passage. But the episode of Pandemonium is intrinsically amplified, a piece of epic expansiveness which does much

more than fulfill the obligations of genre. One may think that
the poet's pleasure in his own performance is nowhere more
evident, while tacit, and implicated in other motives.

The whole composition is spectacular and intensifies the
element of display by the very extravagance of the invention.
We have noted some risks previously taken by balancing
sympathetic closeness and controlled distance, by bringing
together immediate excitement and the discipline of suspended judgment, by the precision of excess combined with
latencies that create the pressure of unformulated questions.
Now Milton involves his "art" in the "adventurous song," as
a contribution to the spectacle, as if he were entering and
mocking a contest to illustrate the art of English poesy. The
presence of the poet in the performance is felt in the imaginative exuberance, and especially in the exercise of control—in
the continuities and discontinuities, in the delays and urgencies and protracted moments of enclosed leisure; felt as he
pauses to direct a playful mischief to the subjects, or as he
takes up prominent moral positions with a deliberate sobri-
ety that would appear to disclaim any intimate relationship
with the flow of dazzling materials; but the control is felt most
of all as he practises an art of concealment that is ostentatiously invisible, to which no fit reader can be indifferent.

We cannot arrest and isolate some of these delicate procedures without a heavy hand, least inappropriate if we begin,
as Milton does, with Mammon. In the portraits of supervising
engineer and architect Milton echoes, with differences, the
singleness of moral attitude sustained in his epic catalogue of
devils. Mammon is in charge, and that is the occasion for
some old-fashioned verses which point the traditional moral
lessons with a four-square humorlessness that seems as
much on display as the sheer superfluousness, in its breathtaking beauty, of Mulciber's fall. Mammon like Belial has no
temple or altar but no lack of "sons" to follow his example of
concentering himself downward in admiration of gold, more
attractive than the "vision beatific." (The reversal of normal
word order in this last phrase manages to make its great traditional weight sound hollow, a pleasure found insubstantial
and dismissed.) Six lines in a row, an example unique, I believe, in Milton, make their pause after the sixth syllable, and
four of the pauses are as heavily obvious as in incompetent
fifteenth-century verse:

> *For treasures better hid. Soon had his crew*
> *Opened into the hill a spacious wound*
> *And digged out ribs of gold. Let none admire*
> *That riches grow in hell; that soil may best*
> *Deserve the precious bane. And here let those*
> *Who boast in mortal things . . . .*
>
> (I, 688–93)

The passage continues with a lesson drawn from the same well-catalogued moral treasury:

> *and wond'ring tell*
> *Of Babel, and the works of Memphian kings,*
> *Learn how their greatest monuments of fame,*
> *And strength and art are easily outdone*
> *By Spirits reprobate, and in an hour*
> *What in an age they with incessant toil*
> *And hands innumerable scarce perform.*
>
> (I, 693–99)

While evoking by historical example the resonances of innumerable lectures on the notorious misdirections of human effort, the style switches from naive to sophisticated. The moral lesson is delivered with a flourish of expansive syntactical energy and rhythm, the work of strength and art, and continuous grace—until the "scarce perform," which concludes with a contrasting touch of asperity and compression. This last note is taken up by the comment which follows the description of the building-in-process. The moral is then delivered with a stylistic flourish in which the expressive energy does not expand but is compressed by brief, multiple reference massed between closely spaced verbs which focus their suggestiveness in a concrete, limited action:[3]

> *Not Babylon,*
> *Nor great Alcairo such magnificence*
> *Equaled in all their glories, to enshrine*
> *Belus or Serapis their gods, or seat*
> *Their kings, when Egypt with Assyria strove*
> *In wealth and luxury.*
>
> (I, 717–22)

This is followed by a glimpse into the interior of the structure and by the noisy entrance of an admiring audience, which provides the digressive opportunity for a biographical note on the architect. Leisurely grace and expansiveness return in the set piece on Mulciber's fall, a composition of exquisite verbal beauty which has won its own distinctive place among the "monuments of fame" produced by the English language. The description is prefaced by an authentication of Mulciber's architectural achievements in heaven and the authorized functions of those structures. The leisurely fall is given out as a false report, a garbled account fathered by a fable, set between two abrupt, bare disclaimers, and concluded by a relentlessly harsh judgment in an appropriate verbal orchestration:

> *Thus they relate,*
> *Erring; for he with this rebellious rout*
> *Fell long before; nor aught availed him now*
> *To have built in heav'n high tow'rs; nor did he scape*
> *By all his engines, but was headlong sent*
> *With his industrious crew to build in hell.*
> *(I, 746–51)*

The moral commentary is direct and straightforward, neither expansive nor compressed, and one cannot relate it to commentary which presents itself in either naive or sophisticated style. The humor, which we may suspect, reveals no internal signals but can be ascribed only to the extraordinary juxtaposition of a slow fictitious fall and a fast actual one, and to the juxtaposition of a pure, self-enclosed, imaginative indulgence and a sweeping condemnation that pointedly ignores the poet's heavenly hand in the "towered structure." The attitude expressed does, however, echo and amplify previous notes of moral judgment, and especially the harsh condemnation that follows a similar passage of digressive illustration, the epic simile comparing Satan's bulk to Leviathan's. The simile is also notable for the slightness of its pretext; in addition, its commanding imagination of the event (the narrative of the benighted skiff anchoring to Leviathan) may be translated into a synoptic history of man and Satan—complete with symbolic anchor, apparently absolute error, a close, threatening atmosphere of anxious watch, and both parties mistaken. In the knotted uncertainties and cross purposes, Satan will be made to serve Providence, and Leviathan, so long as the tale lasts, unwittingly serves the mistaken pilot. But we cannot know whether we are invited to tease out a symbolic interpretation; for the poet, having drawn us into a set story that reads like a parable, breaks it off and reads out a moral condemnation of Satan that turns away from Leviathan and the plight of the lost pilot, who may or may not represent the general case of man "seduced" by Satan. With this simile, and with the fallen angels pictured as "Memphian chivalry" watched "From the safe shore," and with the fall of Mulciber, we are presented with convincing imaginative excess and powerful silences. Whenever a commentary does not seem quite aligned to the poetic occasion from which it derives, or if it has an inclusive air but seems disproportionate or makes omissions, we are left with the desire to ask questions and with the sense that the author's purpose may have anticipated our feeling so.

We have another step to make in this direction when we come to the last lines of the book. Meanwhile—a word indispensable to Milton and a helpful admission of negligence in our efforts to follow his manifold activities—we have had to pass by the actual building of Pandemonium in our pursuit of other matters. Milton's description seems to be based not so much upon the wit of excess as upon a constant matching of the definite and the indefinite. On the one hand we are given a matter-of-fact, circumstantial account, beginning with the volcanic hill, "not far," that to the experienced eye contained the desired metal. The infernal factory uses assembly-line techniques, preparing and forming the metal in co-ordinated stages clearly described—up to a point. On the other hand, certain parts of the process are not for publication and are glossed as "With wondrous art" and "By strange conveyance," and by the splendid simile of the organ, which fills the mind but would not quite serve as a model for reproducing the industrial methods. The wind that furnishes the organ with its building material introduces the rising structure and the end of any definiteness in the account:

> *Rose like an exhalation, with the sound*
> *Of dulcet symphonies and voices sweet.*
> *(I, 711–12)*

The origin of the music as poetic idea may depend on the relationship of Jubal and Tubalcain (reinvented by some modern primitivizers, as in Soviet music imitating the acoustical beauties of the steel foundry and the heart-warming sounds that accompanied the building of the great Dnieper

Dam). Still, Milton expects the reader to share his own preference for unambiguous instrumentation and orchestral positioning; background music of dubious origin ("*with* the sound") is both magic and joke, part of the straight-faced mischief of combining the apparently definite and the pervasively vague.

Meanwhile there is a council announced, with appropriate ceremony and sound, and a new technical problem to be overcome, that of fitting the giant crowd into a "covered field." But room is made for the numberless by marvelously making them small at "the signal giv'n," and the practical accomplishment of infernal magic is trumpeted by the narrative voice: "Behold a wonder!" In the meantime, the lingering pause over the bees, which precedes the "wonder," offers without comment a reflecting glance at the exhibition of technology, magic, music, and wit which collaborate in the building of Pandemonium:

> As bees
> In springtime, when the sun with Taurus rides,
> Pour forth their populous youth about the hive
> In clusters; they among fresh dews and flowers
> Fly to and fro, or on the smoothed plank,
> The suburb of their straw-built citadel,
> New rubbed with balm, expatiate and confer
> Their state affairs.
>
> (I, 768–75)

Time stops, as with the imaginative adventure of hell's marching music, or the series of changes that turns the fallen angels into an image of the drowned Egyptian cavalry, or as with the narrative adventure left suspended of the lost pilot who moors his skiff by the side of Leviathan. Here we are drawn into a pastoral world of self-concerned movement, the orderly business of which it is our pleasure, natural and learned, to be absorbed by. Not until the phrase "their straw-built citadel" ripples the surface are we reminded of Pandemonium and then of the unprecedented aroma of balm in hell. When the mass expands and contracts, like some great diastolic-systolic movement in political multitudes that "expatiate and confer / Their state affairs," the bookish diction is spectacular in its metaphorical precision. Like Satan's shield and spear, the imaginative transfers between great and small are linked to perspective and stimulated consciousness. The bees acting like men are as men acting like bees; both resemble the pulsations of an anxious crowd seen from the distance of height. In the frozen moment we may glimpse reflections of the many passages in which Milton contracts and expands imaginative materials, exercising the range of our vision and our awareness of question, choice, and judgment.

We see the human connections, and recognize the compelling "wonder" of the art to reduce our attention to the confines of a small episode which pretends to be only an illustrative transition to the wonder of solving the problem of infernal spectator space. But the artist who can do these things, and contrive to allow us our glimpses outside the walls of what is immediately happening, can also impose his power to prevent reflection and can make us feel the increased tension in our esthetic experience. The control of tempo is one of the finer sides of Milton's wit and a basic technique of his art. We are carried along by the sweep of the verse and by the press of new narrative materials. From bees to the mention of dwarfs and Pygmies beyond the Himalayas, and then we settle down to the English countryside and its folklore version of the supernatural, the fairy elves who conduct their "midnight revels by a forest side / Or fountain" while, in an appropriate landscape of moonlit illusion, "some belated peasant sees, / Or dreams he sees." Familiar lore, acquired young, teaches how to respond to the pleasure and danger of such a scene:

> *they on their mirth and dance*
> *Intent, with jocund music charm his ear;*
> *At once with joy and fear his heart rebounds.*
> *(I, 786–88)*

Joy and fear, separate and linked, are the double response which would seem to underlie Milton's concept of how to write an epic first book on hell. The lost pilot and the "belated peasant" are the only human figures, though widely separated, brief in appearance, and left dangling in an uncompleted tale, with whom we may identify our own feelings and interests. The pilot, in his landscape of illusion, caught up in the sense of relief passing into anxiety, anticipates the peasant. The fairy elves and the peasant between them represent in brief much of the poem thus far. If we glance ahead, we remember that joy is Adam's first recorded emotion: "With fragrance and with joy my heart o'erflowed" (VIII, 266). If we look still further ahead, Michael tells the fallen Adam that he has come to teach him "True patience, and to temper joy with fear" (XI, 361).

But meanwhile certain of the fallen angels have not been reduced to accommodating size and are not to be compared to anything but themselves:

> *But far within,*
> *And in their own dimensions like themselves,*
> *The great Seraphic Lords and Cherubim*
> *In close recess and secret conclave sat,*
> *A thousand demi-gods on golden seats,*
> *Frequent and full. After short silence then*
> *And summons read, the great consult began.*
> *(I, 792–98)*

The straight statement, with no extrinsic reference, comparison, or comment, is the final novelty Milton invents, and its full effect depends on the context of expectations created by the procedures thus far. One remarkable effect is a surprising variation that suppresses overt moral comment after a long flight of fancy. Milton does not turn on his episode as he did after the lesser amplifications of Leviathan and the fall of Mulciber. Instead, he pretends that the narrative is a truthful account and not a deliberately overwrought fiction, a glittering but sinister bubble, a diversion of much ado about very little. The joke on the democracy of hell and on its imitators does not, of course, need interpretation, but the moral instinct for expression does not always consult the need to interpret. Yet at least some of our esthetic expectation is answered by the extraordinary harshness, the stylistic *asprezza*, that emerges from the deliberate moral neutrality of the opening lines above: their audible arrangement seems to be scored for brass with appropriate punctuation and the *fortissimo* coming at "The great Seraphic Lords and Cherubim."

The confident projection of these lines may be compared with some of the creaking moralistic lines that Milton chose to attach to Mammon:

> *By him first*
> *Men also, and by his suggestion taught,*
> *Ransacked the center, and with impious hands*

Rifled the bowels óf their mother earth
For treasures better hid.

(I, 684–88)

(The marks above are to indicate how Milton has leaned on the meter at prominently weak places, as if to acknowledge equal debt to poetic indignation and poetic license.) The clumsy lines on Mammon are an obvious joke by a master poet ostentatiously playing with his craft; the humor is not, however, directed at a single, stationary target, but is distributed and shared, like some highly wrought piece of miming which delights with outward satisfactions while creating inward attachments and questions. The lines on the unminiaturized fallen angels satisfy in that we can compose our own answer to the obvious restraint of what is not said: the answer of the political joke. But what we supply has been anticipated and is more like a bait of red herring—an easy answer to a flourish of the unstated, which persons of refined humor may enjoy as an intimate joke on the art of joking, and which entertains chiefly by leaving the real questions exactly where they were.

The privilege of the poet to keep his counsel is the employment of the critic; if he borrows more than a little of that privilege he should be writing his own poem or resigning from office. Let us try to look back at the main issues we have been treating. Milton's hell presents the deterioration of truth, for the most part expressed indirectly by what is wrong and perverse, but there is direct support of the main point by frequent reference to traditional moral thought; at the same time intense moments of imaginative sympathy surprise, enrich, and complicate but do not diminish the main emphasis. What is great even in decline is treated with suitable dignity, though the grandeur is more poetic than substantial, art exerting itself to produce shimmering triumphs in which the hand of the artist alternates between ostentation and invisibility. There is perhaps a hint of residual mockery, if we are receptive, in that description of the infernal spectators who are divided into the class of those who admire the work and those the architect. The episode of Pandemonium is presented as the supreme novelty, with a large measure of joy provided by the esthetic experience. We are excited and stretched by the unexpected, satisfied by the immediate rightness of the expression while feeling the questions we cannot answer and sometimes cannot ask, but we confidently anticipate new pleasures while never being able to predict the shape of their coming. The esthetic delight is made of its own stuff, *sui generis*, and leads nowhere, a splendid, static exuberance. There is no "Sense of new joy" related to outward events, no choice, no trial—except the one event, which is left dangling and seems to be the symbolic clue to everything else, the simultaneous joy and fear experienced by the "belated peasant." But the reader may feel well tried. He has been taught by the poet to endure questions without expecting full and instant answers, and has experienced some of the first lessons in the literary task of learning "True patience."

Let us now consider a second major example, the sudden novelty of Adam's full disclosure of the passion he has discovered in his love for Eve. This novelty, unlike the episode of Pandemonium, does not have the exhilarating air of entertainment; the issue is real, and the delayed climax all at once feels closer. The novelty cannot come as complete invention, as at the beginning of the history of hell; we are too far into the poem and its lines of preparation. The surprises of time are less free to assume unexpected combinations, for though this is an authentic beginning, something new in the world that is being told for the first time, between it and the reader lies an imposing history of thought, comment, and experience. It will be the poet's task to keep the perspective right, to prevent the foreground, with its familiar certainties of fallen experience, from slipping into the background. Milton wants the background to be open, with no shadows except those of his own deliberate making, the intimations that suggest potential directions but do not commit. This novelty, unlike the matter of Pandemonium, must engage the truths of traditional thought and must bring the issue of choice into view.

The immediate foreground, the intervening history which must be kept from assuming the perspectival influence of a background, is clear enough in its main outline. The place of sexual passion in the fall was a subject widely discussed under the stimulating shelter of scriptural reticence. Christian commentators were in general agreement that there could be no libidinal desire in Paradise, and that this blessing was lost with the expulsion. Conservative opinion found it reasonable to conclude that Adam and Eve remained virgins while in Paradise. Rabbinical comment, when it regarded the expulsion as but one of many human crises, was less inhibited. In addition, theories deriving from folklore, from the influences of Platonic dualism, from apocryphal and other esoteric sources, attached a floating body of sexual mythology to the bare biblical story. All of this, however, orthodox opinion could dismiss as unfounded and philosophically irresponsible, the diversions of frivolous *fabulantes.* The instincts of sober speculators were much freer to express themselves by pondering how the business of being fruitful would have been managed if Adam and Eve had remained innocent. Milton has Adam anticipate some of these oddities of angelic reproduction when he laments that God did not people earth as heaven "without feminine."

In spite of the need of theologians to uphold the sanctity of marriage, for secular reasons and for mystical reasons signifying the dignity of the church and the relations of the Trinity, it seemed wiser to postpone the consummation of marriage until after the expulsion, which was probably not too long to wait and perhaps only a few hours. But even if, as some held, Adam and Eve waited in abstinent grief for a hundred years before Cain was conceived, this did not wholly diminish the emphasis on the serious problem of sexual passion. Nor did centuries of praise for virginity, abstinence, mortification, and other values lessen the vigilance of commentators toward the discreetly veiled meanings of Scripture. Even minds of rigorous purity were prone to suspect that when Eve gave Adam the forbidden fruit and he ate, the woman exerted a latent influence for which there was a disastrous overabundance of subsequent evidence. Sober thinkers would strive to maintain a proper perspective, and to observe the rules of theological reasoning and chronology, but there could be no doubt that women were not only subject to libidinal desire of frightening proportions but were the stimulating object of masculine desire.

Milton clearly breaks with the older conservatism in making Adam and Eve married lovers who are nevertheless innocent. He therefore has to present them in a state that is not without some inherent mystery and will require calculated and varied efforts if he is to be persuasive. He makes firm but sparing use of direct statement, of which the hymn to wedded love is the most powerful and sustained example. Less sparing are the indirect supports of affecting poetic ornamentation and the steady example of natural dignity in their relationship. On the other side, he cultivates negative support by the dissonances of occasional reference to the life of fallen sexuality, and by the shocking contrast of the scene he produces after the fall, illustrating the lasciviousness which did not exist before. But since he undertakes to maintain the sanctity of marriage in a literal and actual presentation that is intended not to obviate, but to include the more respectable virtual meanings of the symbolic traditions, he cannot indefinitely postpone or avoid the subject of sexual passion. Indeed, fit readers acquainted with the issue and its history might well feel a tightening of suspense during the long interval, from early in the fourth to late in the eighth book, before the subject comes up directly.

First let us review some of the deliberate background of the episode, background Milton himself provides. Adam's first formal trial was to discover and express his human incompleteness. With the help of dialogue and a divine questioner he reasoned out his need, the gift which God wanted him to name and justify. In the dialogue Adam expressed knowledge, self-knowledge, and the reasoning of love, but not easily. He was tentative, groping, yet persistent in trying to discover and explain his need for a kind of love that had no exact precedents in the universe, that was an idea existing only in God's mind and without an image yet. The result was Eve, whom God called, "Thy wish exactly to thy heart's desire," and Adam called the "fairest" of all God's gifts, or, when it came time to excuse his actions, "thy perfect gift." Though Milton's fable is charming and graceful, it is also a rigorous exhibition of capacities which, once they are demonstrated, serve as a measure of human responsibility. There may be no retreat from intellectual and moral recognition; once it is shown to exist it may not be declined. The principle governs matters of truth, novelty, and choice, and governs the poet in his own freedom and in the larger freedom he would justify.

In the underworld of "No light, but rather darkness visible" Milton could indulge his art, confident in his reader's unimpaired access to underlying truths and in his capacity to learn the right lessons from the unprecedented displays to which he is treated. The freedoms Milton takes are mostly artistic ones, which have their own hard rules but give pleasure when they seem to be broken but are not, or are instead transcended, or seem to be made by the writer himself as he pleases, yet satisfy our immediate responses and reflective judgment. Standing on earth, however, Milton is less free to invent occurrences which lead nowhere, which have no outward relationship to truth and choice. What Milton binds himself to do with his materials, their expression, and their order, his characters must attempt to do with their thoughts, feelings, and experiences. They are governed by what they show themselves to have understood—as Satan demonstrates at length in his soliloquies.

The first human emotion felt is joy, and it is one of Milton's boldest assertions of Providence. Milton accepts the challenge and the consequences of endowing original human nature with a primary intuition of joy. He has made a deliberate choice which expresses both his long-range narrative intentions and his personal vision of human nature and its destiny. The joy Adam feels is a divine gift unasked for; in acknowledging his possession he assumes conscious responsibility for its preservation and use. But to speak more strictly, Adam's first experiences after creation precede his discovery of language, and the sense of joy wells up before it has a name. Though telling a true story, Adam must take the poet's way and create a fiction in order to reproduce in words what he experienced before he tried to speak. His choice commits him, and the emotion that in retrospect, in a serious fiction, is named joy can be nothing else.

The first impromptu exercise in language moves from lyric naming to reasoning, as Adam validates Raphael's great assertion that intuitive and discursive reasoning (angelic or human) differ but in degree, not in kind. Adam raises, shows an intuitive need to raise, and decisively answers the question of his origin:

> *Not of myself; by some great Maker then,*
> *In goodness and in power pre-eminent.*
> *Tell me, how may I know him, how adore,*
> *From whom I have that thus I move and live,*
> *And feel that I am happier than I know?*
> *(VIII, 278–82)*

So the first emotion leads to a demonstration of ontological argument and then to the discovery of the first ethical imperative, gratitude, which coincides with the beginning of religious response. When joy expressing itself through reason recognizes the human need for gratitude, that acceptance constitutes the premise of an "argument" the rational consequences of which must justify themselves in the actions of all concerned. The poet must justify himself by his management of the story, which is an office of immense power limited chiefly by the restraints he chooses, and these must be the right ones if his power is to possess the virtues of authority, which the reader must freely grant. And the story teller must justify his own ways in showing the character's convincing freedom to manage and answer for the life he acts out.

We soon learn that joy is free to move in other directions, as Milton quickens the tempo of his narrative. Two hundred and fifty lines later Adam is confiding to Raphael the difference between the other delights of Paradise and the passion he feels for Eve. When he tries to reason about *this* joy he produces hypothetical explanations not inappropriate to the "commotion strange" of passion for the first time discovered. We shall need the whole speech before us:

> *Thus I have told thee all my state,*
>   *and brought*
> *My story to the sum of earthly bliss*
> *Which I enjoy, and must confess to find*
> *In all things else delight indeed, but such*
> *As used or not, works in the mind no change,*
> *Nor vehement desire, these delicacies*
> *I mean of taste, sight, smell, herbs, fruits,*
>   *and flow'rs,*
> *Walks, and the melody of birds; but here*
> *Far otherwise, transported I behold,*
> *Transported touch; here passion first I felt,*
> *Commotion strange, in all enjoyments else*
> *Superior and unmoved, here only weak*
> *Against the charm of beauty's powerful glance.*
> *Or Nature failed in me, and left some part*
> *Not proof enough such object to sustain,*
> *Or from my side subducting, took perhaps*
> *More than enough; at least on her bestowed*
> *Too much of ornament, in outward show*
> *Elaborate, of inward less exact.*
> *For well I understand in the prime end*
> *Of Nature her th'inferior, in the mind*
> *And inward faculties, which most excel;*

In outward also her resembling less
His image who made both, and less expressing
The character of that dominion giv'n
O'er other creatures; yet when I approach
Her loveliness, so absolute she seems
And in herself complete, so well to know
Her own, that what she wills to do or say
Seems wisest, virtuousest, discreetest, best;
All higher knowledge in her presence falls
Degraded, wisdom in discourse with her
Loses discount'nanced, and like folly shows;
Authority and reason on her wait,
As one intended first, not after made
Occasionally; and to consummate all,
Greatness of mind and nobleness their seat
Build in her loveliest, and create an awe
About her, as a guard angelic placed.
                    (VIII, 521–59)

In that intellect that first discovers gratitude the movements of knowledge are beautifully simple and sure. Intuitive and discursive knowledge are at one with each other and with feeling; even when the limits of knowledge are reached, a crucial test, feeling remains a reliable guide: "And feel that I am happier than I know." But in reasoning about the joy of passion knowledge makes an exorbitant display of itself, offering to explain what is not understood, the mysterious weakness felt. Adam insists on his knowledge and on the place of knowledge, but as preface to a moving demonstration of transposed roles in a newly invented fiction for which there are not yet names in Paradise: "so absolute she seems . . . so well to know . . . Seems wisest . . . All higher knowledge in her presence falls . . . like folly shows . . . As one intended first."

The limits of knowledge are quickly transferred to the guidance of feeling—not in the simple, spontaneous way of "And feel that I am happier than I know," but in a self-conscious, complex, and hypothetical way. Under the privilege of what is imagined, feeling would seem to subvert knowledge while taking upon itself the prerogatives of knowledge. Though in a fiction, a friendly and intimate confession, not of what should be, not even of what actually is, but instead, a candid, unselfcritical effort to express how the experience makes him feel, Adam has exhibited an ominous human capacity for inversion. What he feels for Eve may be called a number of things, though these are as yet forbidden by the governing laws of the story. What one cannot miss, however, is the authorized background of Milton's own making: the first emotion, responding to many objects and leading the whole man by a process of reason to concentrate on source and to feel gratitude; in contrast, this emotion, concentrated on one object, makes the task of reason that of trying to explain weakness and the sense of inner division ("some part / Not proof enough such object to sustain"), with the result that reason turns on itself, both declaring and acting out, though still in a fiction, its own inadequacy.

We know the simple answer. Eve too is part of the benevolent order, to which the untroubled response is gratitude. But her creation *is* special and separate; she is made incidentally from a part of Adam's body but essentially from a collaboration in dialogue between the eternal mind and Adam's mind in its first sustained trial. When Adam reasons out the need for Eve, it is an act of self-knowledge, "Expressing well the spirit within thee free." She is at once part of the order that leads to gratitude and part of the order of trial by freedom, a crucial test of reason and feeling and their limits, at once object and subject, "thy other self / Thy wish exactly to thy heart's desire."

The answer is simple because the concept of gratitude is basic in Milton's religious anthropology. He inherits the concept along with its traditional support, which is of the right kind for his enterprise. The support is there, and he can formally disregard it as merely marking intellectual agreement, and the systematic extension and refinement of a truth so plain and essential that the first man discovers it for himself at the beginning, in his authoritative first encounter with life. The intellectual necessity of gratitude can be demonstrated by religious intuition or by the apparatus of religious thought, which can also explore the connections with pride and the alternatives to turning wholly toward God. Milton would expect these implications to exert a reinforcing pressure upon his decorum of silence, which obeys the laws of his narrative truth and is thus privileged to show the idea at its source, a narrative equivalent of Socrates' vision of the ideas. Nor should one fail to notice in a writer who values order and priority that God's first recorded comments on man mention gratitude just after obedience and before freedom.

What is of special value to the narrative artist, however, is that gratitude is both an intellectual and a moral virtue, a free obligation recognized by the mind and felt by the will. When all is well, gratitude represents a concord of intellect and will, a symbol of human integrity—as obedience in the test of the forbidden fruit was traditionally understood as a symbol of free will. But when all is not well, the will is revealed as powerless to command a feeling that should be, like joy, natural and easy.

This description has led, as the issue itself does, toward the climax that Milton foreshadows, which involves the ultimate prohibition of the forbidden tree. Adam's discovery of passion is a crucial, balancing scene which first brings a new force into view, a feeling which threatens the concord of mind and will. An answer to the new force of sexual passion cannot be simple in the way the answer of gratitude is simple. Even the angel speaks with some asperity and excess, and anticipates not only future human arguments but some of the troubled feeling which creeps into them. In a moral crisis he too must analyze integrity and separate it into higher and lower functions, counseling a defense in which choosing and denial are more prominent than they have been thus far in the human drama. His advice, though angelic, does not achieve the authority of a great original; it is no better or worse than wise men since have said. He analyzes Adam's error well enough, but he fails to find a positive function for man's "Sense of new joy." True love ascends to heavenly love and is rational, he declares; the opposite is "sunk in carnal pleasure." There seems to be no middle ground for action, or even dignity.

Adam's answer does, with stubborn dignity, defend the marriage bed and its "mysterious reverence." But otherwise he agrees with the angel by offering his own personal account of what is "Attractive, human, rational" in his love for Eve. His account is by no means a reversal or revision; he summarizes what has been amply shown to be true, but he pointedly omits a defense of passion. As for that, Adam agrees in principle with the angel, and he offers the defense that he has been only telling what he feels, not what he thinks, and he provides a brief summary to prove that he knows what and how to think:

> Yet these subject not; I to thee disclose
> What inward thence I feel, not therefore foiled,
> Who meet with various objects, from the sense

Variously representing; yet still free,
Approve the best, and follow what I approve.
(VIII, 607–11)

It is an effective speech, though it unfortunately anticipates a famous quotation that illustrates how easily the truth in words can be perverted.[4] One may also mark how firm and clear Adam's verbal posture is and how it differs from the opening of his long disclosure on passion, where three vague references to "here," contrasted with "all things else," "all enjoyments else," are anchored with a retrospective intensity in "the sum of earthly bliss," the experiences of the nuptial night. When he told his story he cloaked these experiences in a splendid ceremony of nature celebrating the event, but now he will try to tell part of the other story.

Innocent love is rational, and sexual love in Paradise is innocent but may have the potentiality of irrational passion. The story asks us to believe this as part of the conditions of freedom and trial. What Adam *feels*, the story asks us to believe, is an intellectual error which chiefly consists in his overvaluing a single aspect of his experience—or, as Milton composes the ambiguity, in Adam's appearing to do so in his effort to understand and express "What inward thence I feel." The issue is plainly difficult for fallen readers to grasp, as prudent theologians anticipated. But Milton does not shirk the efforts *his* choice has committed him to, which requires that Adam try to express what he feels in terms that borrow from, and threaten, what he knows. Adam declares that passion, unlike other pleasures, "works in the mind . . . change," and that he is "transported," by sight as well as by touch. In attributing to passion a mental value Adam anticipates the language of ecstasy—as Adam's sleep during the creation of Eve could be interpreted by exegetes as a type of mystic vision. Milton turns away from such speculations, though he is a master of turning away while borrowing to transpose. He would appear to link Adam's present account with his earlier waking dreams, but now Adam takes a further step and rationalizes an exchange of priorities. Without the pressure of a necessary moral choice, but as a free response, Adam has been practicing (though perversely) what the angel's counter-argument in its own way also insists on—the separating of higher and lower functions in terms that approach rejection.[5] (In a calmer mood, in his authoritative exposition of the chain

of being, Raphael optimistically presented the normal order
as one in which higher functions completely assimilated
lower, with no sense of threat or rejection "If not depraved
from good.")

In retreat Adam reiterates a ruling principle of rational
ethics:

> *Who meet with various objects, from the sense*
> *Variously representing; yet still free,*
> *Approve the best, and follow what I approve.*
> *(VIII, 609–11)*

The issue is left more inconclusive than Adam's expression,
which benefits from the author's power to digest and concentrate traditional thought so that it rings like a pronouncement from the source. The episode has demonstrated neither
the innocence nor the guilt of passion, but only its potential
danger. Here again Milton would expect the traditional
thought of subsequent history to apply pressure to the
episode, while nevertheless being prevented, by the authorized fact of Adam's innocence, from reaching any final judgment. As the historians and theorists of "heroic love" might
have diagnosed the case, Adam's danger does not lie in the
understanding itself, nor in the direct effect of passion, nor in
the imagination entirely. The characteristic symptom is that
blurring of judgment to which the understanding is suscepti-
ble when not in its own power but is in part being used by the
neighboring faculty of imagination, which exhibits a familiar
tendency to encroach on reason—as indicated by this effort
to analyze an effect which it finds moving and mysterious.
Adam's attempt to explain himself is not a passionate speech,
in no way resembling what he called his "pleaded reason" in
the first courtship of Eve. It is rather an imaginative speech
consciously trying to explain, conscious of awkward difficulties, noting them and straining to overcome them—by a candid translation of feeling into a knowledge of feeling, not only
"disclosing" but striving to interpret the "inward thence." It
is an experiment in intimate expression that does not succeed, except in exhibiting symptoms that may well cause a
"contracted brow" in any detached listener.

In spite of the possible impropriety in Adam's asking for a
reciprocal confidence, his question concerning angelic love,
the question does bring into focus something both Adam and
Raphael have been distorting. The angel, though blushing,

relaxes and admits the basic truth which he has been suppressing and Adam has been exaggerating: that physical love *is* pure. There is no happiness without love:

> *Whatever pure thou in the body enjoy'st*
> *(And pure thou wert created) we enjoy*
> *In eminence, and obstacle find none*
> *Of membrane, joint, or limb, exclusive bars;*
> *Easier than air with air, if Spirits embrace,*
> *Total they mix, union of pure with pure*
> *Desiring; nor restrained conveyance need*
> *As flesh to mix with flesh, or soul with soul.*
>   *(VIII, 622–29)*

It is a masterly touch of narrative placement, the point of agreement coming as an affirmation, *after* the formal statement and counter-statement, and from the angelic mouth which has been counseling choice and negative discriminations. Raphael presents the most surprisingly sensual passage in the poem, unique in subject, style, and in the confident reach of majestic casualness, celebrating union as union, under the comprehensive sanction of happiness.

The angel's disclosure, whatever it owes to the traditions of exotic thought, is an astounding novelty, in itself and in its timing. The heavenly experience clearly transcends the issue of choice and is a splendid excess, perhaps like the building of Pandemonium, but expressing joy without fear; indeed, without any discernible limitation. An unlimited sensuousness not only exceeds the concepts of union by material body or immaterial soul, but offers metaphorical bridges that disappear in the brilliant negatives ("exclusive bars," "restrained conveyance") that gesture toward definition yet leave the limited human imagination with some "glorious nothing" to work upon. The account is brief and broken off. There is no room to refer to other celestial pleasures duly mentioned elsewhere. Has the angel offered his counter version of "the sum" of heavenly bliss, though not to be contrasted with "all things else," "all enjoyments else"? We are plainly not invited to speculate about inward and outward faculties, wisdom, or the comparative joys of the beatific vision. We may, however, see a baffling humor in the angelic revelation to the newlywed awkwardly trying to give a rational shape to his inward feelings.[6]

As often, so often as to constitute a major unasked critical question, Milton permits no time to reflect on questions he does not quite raise, but seems to prefer that we wonder whether and how they might be raised. Nor is this the only reticence of the episode.

After Raphael's long narrations of universal affairs, closely followed by Adam's "thoughts abstruse" directed toward astronomy, Raphael demonstrates the limits of human knowledge and counsels joy directed toward Paradise and Eve: "Think only what concerns thee and thy being." Adam grasps the point and demonstrates his recognition by spelling out the lesson in some detail:

> But apt the mind or fancy is to rove
> Unchecked, and of her roving is no end;
> Till warned, or by experience taught, she learn
> That not to know at large of things remote
> From use, obscure and subtle, but to know
> That which before us lies in daily life,
> Is the prime wisdom; what is more, is fume,
> Or emptiness, or fond impertinence,
> And renders us in things that most concern
> Unpractised, unprepared, and still to seek.
> *(VIII, 188–97)*

His own story then follows and ends as we have seen, not without "roving" of "mind or fancy," and not without some "subtle" concentration on a practical matter of daily life, as if it were a thing "remote" to be known "at large." As for his having gained experience and preparation from the angel's "warning," that is left as an open question to join other questions.

The issue of trial and obedience, always present but modest in its proportions of external emphasis, now approaches its formal crisis, and the established principle is that the danger, as the crucial decision, lies "within." The chain of preparation has been subtle, flexible, and unhurried. There has been ample time for long stories and a leisure befitting Paradise and the dignity of human choice. Now the tempo and the intensity are suddenly raised, and a serious, unresolved issue emerges—at the very end of the angel's mission. "But I can now no more," Raphael says, breaking off his description of angelic love and pointing to "the parting sun" as the signal for departure. There is, however, time for a parting benediction which turns into a summary exhortation:

> *Be strong, live happy, and love, but first of all*
> *Him whom to love is to obey.*
> (VIII, 633–34)

To which he adds a brief warning on passion and temptation, and his own encouraging pledge of personal involvement. Adam's answer, with no impropriety at all, passes over the guest's final words, and the grateful host fulfills his larger obligation with a comprehensive courtesy of perfect grace. We note the proper fulfillment and its excellence, and admire the narrative skill which has so politely arranged the leaving of things unsaid. This joins other reticences, as Raphael's "But I can now no more" also suggests meanings not attached to time. We are left with open questions and an issue closing in.

A strange quality in Adam's speech on passion is so well adapted to the subject and the action that one hesitates over recognition and naming. In the excitement of his novel effort Adam tends to put himself into a state of feeling that resembles and nurtures what he would express, and we may hear, or dream we hear, some intimations of a kind of recklessness which has hitherto, with differences in scale and duration, been the exclusive property of Satan's expression. There is an important difference in degree, and we do not for a moment doubt Adam's sincerity. But he is *acting*, feeling for the first time in the poem a need to act in order to say the unexpressed, and he must do so without a poet's veteran detachment in telling "Things unattempted," and especially the story that happens to someone else. Adam has felt no such need before, and we have heard nothing that might be interpreted as a flush of embarrassed boldness, a kind of exhilaration that will characterize a period of his fallen speech and is not, quite, legitimate to pry into now. Milton has taken care to frustrate such inquiry by the context he has created and managed, but one may also believe that he has managed to introduce the subliminal suggestion.

Other questions, difficult to raise but uncomfortable to suppress once the suggestion of analogy has been recognized, are these: Do the unions of angelic and human love, unlike reasoning, differ in kind or but in degree? Is Raphael's speech, for all its intimacy of revelation, a dazzling discouragement, a reminder of human limits emphasizing, like the lecture on astronomy, the bounds of human experience and the wisdom of not seeking remote knowledge? Or is the speech intended to encourage, by a glimpse of ecstatic privilege, the patience of waiting with obedience until the human promotion to spirit may be granted? Nor may one utterly dismiss a possible middle ground of trial, which may or may not involve an angelic miscalculation which overstimulates and is both like and unlike Eve's dream. The weight of optimism in the poem asserts multiple authoritative correspondences between heaven and earth; as long as the harmony holds, differences are those of degree, not kind. In counterpoise, the single issue of obedience, resting on a single prohibition, but with many inherent connections, compresses all the potentialities of radical difference. In a narrative context the main lines of which are simple and clear we nevertheless find a density like that of myth. The clarity by no means discourages interpretation, and cleverness can produce good arguments, but not an argument that will contain and resolve all the possibilities. We do not find an obscurity as in "things remote," or a subtlety like the reasonings of logic. What is shadowed forth may perhaps bear some suggestive resemblance to mysteries of the human heart—a darkness not quite visible, but a background against which the acting out of events can be made clear.

We shall not be able to say that passion is a direct cause of the fall, or that the "union of pure with pure / Desiring" is a misleading ideal. The evidence revealed by Adam's speech cannot be ignored and cannot be held against him in advance. Milton will be scrupulous in demonstrating the sufficiency of Adam's understanding, which has fumbled with questions before, and with answers. God did not make him perfect, but only "just and right . . . though free." Speculative theology deduced impressive lists of the blessings lost with Paradisal innocence. Among these one may be of particular appeal to a reader, not engaged in a *summa* but only in trying to hold together the materials of truth, novelty, and choice—the capacity of unfallen intelligence to shape doubt and suspend judgment toward uncertain things.

III.

The Satanic Background

This chapter will concentrate on the Satan who speaks in soliloquy and whose internal life is further represented by the descriptive and narrative language the poet invents for that purpose. The demonstration is, I trust, interesting for itself, as the character and role of the antagonist are interesting. In this part of the story, no small advantage, we may also witness a full display of Milton's mastery of dramatic language—the art of expressing inner conflicts, the shifting disguises, blurred suspensions, and brief clarifications, the crosscurrents and tidal movements, the protean shapes imposed upon a fixed structure of reality which cannot be obliterated and which reveals itself as ultimately governing from within and without. Behind Milton's art lies everything he learned from his alert reading in previous poets and dramatists, and from the traditions of thought which explained in theory and practice the nature and actions of the soul in response to immediate and ultimate forces. His major philosophical grounds are the Platonic traditions that relate individual justice to the harmony of the universe, that declare the inner faculties to be attuned to external truth and to be oriented toward a vision of the good. A basic law of the moral life, tenacious in Western thought and indispensable to all the older dramas of the soul, is the Socratic law that evil requires the ignorance which lies in self-deception, and that no man does ill without practicing upon his own reason, commonly by promoting some lesser but more immediate good.

In presenting Satan's inner conflicts Milton can make a full display, subtle and complex but without the careful shadings and restraints necessary in the presentation of Adam and Eve still innocent. As the first two books of the poem serve in part to educate the reader in initial ways, the unrestricted presentation of Satan's inner life serves to introduce the reader to innocent human nature. The progressive development Satan exhibits in part precedes the introduction of Adam and Eve, and can act as a kind of detached accompaniment to what they then say and do. After the fall Satan still serves, with some crucial differences.

If we concentrate on the language Milton attaches to Satan, we can improve our sensitivity to the language of Adam and Eve, through which the poet must attempt to convey some unprecedented experiences. What I hope to accomplish indirectly in this chapter is to clarify in advance an important use of Satan which Milton conceived as an answer to certain technical problems in presenting the story of Adam and Eve. I shall state the main point but not try to argue it; in the next chapter the point will be treated as a kind of critical premise to illustrate various methods of Milton's narrative. The acceptability of my premise concerning Milton's conceptual "answer" will need to rely on whatever support is generated by the critical interpretation and its degree of dependence on the premise. (Needless to say, I did not invent this method of critical reasoning, which the veteran reader will not find unusual.)

The point is this: as Milton chooses to tell the human story at the center of the epic he must prevent the foreground of the reader's fallen experience from becoming the background against which the human actions are to be interpreted. Some of the simple contrasts between original innocence and fallen nature are a necessary part of the story and are not to be restrained; Milton requires no special controls beyond those of his acquired artistic discipline to keep his poem from wandering into the soft excesses of nostalgia and sentimentality. More dangerous, however, are those potential similarities between present and original human nature which the story needs to *suggest* for its own purposes, which stimulate our interest; at the same time the governing rules of the story impose upon such similarities—though any context may be content to do no more than tactfully imply—distinctions and restraints.[1] If these similarities are taken as actual, if they are allowed to guide our understanding of the free actions that are still innocent, the weight of the significance and the very telling of the story that Milton intends will be undermined.

To control the foreground Milton punctuates descriptions of life in the Garden with contrasting references to the ways of the fallen world, but chiefly to emphasize the distinctness and the reality of innocence. He may narrow the gap between the two worlds for purposes of instructive tension, but the gap remains inviolate; otherwise, its narrowing would not produce the authentic tension required for a long story. Without an unbridged gap which one may look down into as well as consciously look across, but not leap over, we should miss the exceptional pleasures of a serious fiction and settle for some premature satisfactions of a lower sort. Milton expected his capable reader to remember the particular difficulties of the story he was reading, and not to seize upon opportunities for shallow simplification—not, for instance, to indulge a sense of superiority to Adam by the direct application of later knowledge to events before the fall. If the reader is tempted to abridge his full fictional freedom—which includes both the range of his identification with Adam and the privilege of separation which the story variously controls to deepen understanding—then he will find himself wandering in another story, where his wrong choices will discover the need for a retrospective clarification, or he must like Satan keep trying to make a rival story valid.[2]

To control the background Milton has, in addition to minor devices, the major example of Satan, who serves, within the story, to forestall the reader's facile interposing of his own knowledge of evil. The universal expert is there, pioneering and struggling in person, acting out a fully developed background in which his real differences from Adam and Eve endow the potential similarities with narrative excitement while still preserving degrees of distance which the unwary reader, taking himself instead of Satan as the measure of things, may fail to do.

In presenting innocence the narrative poet must work within a limited range and quality of experience. That he has made the most of his imaginative opportunity is one of the obvious triumphs of the poem. But that great success also benefits from the support of lesser inventions, difficult to come by and requiring an order of genius that Milton seems to have understood well and worked hard to achieve. The details will be part of the exhibition of the next chapter, but I speak

here only of the Satanic background: before the fall Milton
can magnify the limited human action against that background, stressing the potential implications of similarity
while sustaining the explicit difference; after the fall he can
exploit his opportunity by developing and varying his open
use of the Satanic analogy.

The introduction to Book IV, the arrival of Satan on earth,
the feeling of spent original impetus, the need for a new beginning that emerges amidst the assault of external beauty,
inner hesitation, and the strenuous effort of review—all signal clearly that the Satan of Book IV has entered a new stage.
So has the poem. Satan is now alone and for the first time feels
himself alone. He must do most of his talking to himself. He
must listen, observe, and plan, either in disguise or in hiding.

The credentials that Satan brings into the Garden include,
besides his demonstrated mastery of disguise, his fixed desire
to destroy and his nimble determination to adapt himself to
any shape or circumstances that will bring him closer to his
end. The author may then further exploit the fictional advantage he has obtained by what he has demonstrated in the
development of the character thus far. Satan will, with minor
grumbling, adapt himself to the narrative circumstances. He
has no other course if he is to persevere and hope to succeed.
Either he must have another story (not Milton's) or he must
descend from the imaginative heights and privileges that he
has enjoyed. But Milton is in no hurry to "degrade" Satan or
to ruin "fable and old song" for the sake of moral or sacred
truths. The "new" Satan has to talk to himself, as never before, and cannot conceal the peculiar problems of the habitual
orator trying to tell the truth to himself.

Milton does not need much room before his new effects
begin to work upon us. At the same time the old Satan sends
up not a few of his old signals, and we are reminded of echoes
transposed and of potentialities passed over before but now
ready to emerge. What is absolutely new is the tone of confession, and the Biblical phrases imply attitudes of religious
praise and gratitude:

> *Ah wherefore! He deserved no such return*
> *From me, whom he created what I was*
> *In that bright eminence, and with his good*
> *Upbraided none; nor was his service hard.*
> *(IV, 42–45)*

Praise and gratitude were easy and right, but good turned into ill and produced malice. The tone of confession becomes one of detached self-analysis:

> *lifted up so high*
> *I sdained subjection, and thought one step higher*
> *Would set me highest, and in a moment quit*
> *The debt immense of endless gratitude,*
> *So burthensome still paying, still to owe . . . .*
> *(IV, 49–53)*

When I break the quotation thus, the common description of the vice of pride seems to dominate, but the real subject is the failure of gratitude.

Satan has the intellectual and moral endowment to produce a distinguished account of successful gratitude, and he goes on to attribute his own failure to a lapse of memory and understanding:

> *Forgetful what from him I still received,*
> *And understood not that a grateful mind*
> *By owing owes not, but still pays, at once*
> *Indebted and discharged; what burden then?*
> *(IV, 54–57)*

The language is beautifully turned, but even when moral wisdom sounds graceful, eloquent, and easy, we may still want to ask questions. Satan's eloquence flowers, and he remembers what he forgot and understands what he "understood not." Does that insight, as well as its expression, postdate his fall? If the author has not himself suffered a lapse, then surely the character is caught up in some strange internal complication. We can believe that in heaven Satan forgot what he knew, but not that he has, since the fall, come to understand what he is now expressing—especially since he has deepened his concept of gratitude almost in the next breath. Gratitude is presented as a moral virtue that fails when the rational controls, whether of understanding or memory, fail. Yet a moment before, when Satan was analyzing the causes of his error, the demonstration of failure was presented in language charged with feeling:

> *The debt immense of endless gratitude,*
> *So burthensome still paying, still to owe.*
> *(IV, 52–53)*

Gratitude is one of the virtues that cannot be fulfilled by reason and will. It must be both meant and felt, and it will be less incomplete if it is only felt. If one does not feel gratitude one can at best understand the obligations and one's failure. Satan's "revised" understanding brings forward a piece of enigmatic wisdom; the anguished helplessness beautifully expressed could point toward tragic awareness and struggle, or the authoritative ring of the statement could itself be a substitute for further personal effort. When gratitude is thought about and analyzed by Satan, it is *felt* as an insupportable burden. When it is remembered and "understood," the speaker is then bound to a present state that must choose between alternative actions. One clear action would involve turning back in full acknowledgment of the old failure. Nothing in Satan's authoritative praise of successful gratitude seems transitional to the groping difficulties of beginning again.

The first two books of *Paradise Lost* are not lacking in evidence that the fallen archangel suffers from inner division. Whether we like to hear it said or not, we can see for ourselves that he is "Vaunting aloud, but racked with deep despair." But only with Book IV does Milton begin to develop the potentialities of Satan's inner condition, and the first display consists of the gaps and exchanges between knowledge and feeling.[3] Milton chose the first case well. Gratitude is a particularly sensitive moral virtue and is under extreme pressure when related to the opposing desire for complete independence latent in pride. Satan's demonstration is reflective, a critical account of what happened, but with some immediacies that suggest re-enactment. When he "feels" gratitude as unbearably hateful but "thinks" it a desirable, self-evident good, he is reconstructing an imaginative origin of evil. At the birth of Sin he experienced vertiginous movements that signaled loss of orientation and self-control. That gives us one valuable mythic version. But the mysterious origin one may speculate perhaps, might have come this way too, by whatever disruption first unbalanced the effortless unity of knowledge and feeling, so that the more he then thought about gratitude the less he was able to feel it. Indeed, the intemperateness of the intellectual separation shows how one can turn any accepted obligation into a "debt immense" by arresting it in a thought. A similar act converts eternity into a condition where anything may be felt as "endless."

The issue of gratitude comes early in the speech and is dropped. What continues, however, is the new demonstration of how conflicts emerge in Satan's language and how they are resolved. At a surface level he has explained and corrected the failure of gratitude. It is no burden at all, and he can proceed with his inventory:

> *O had his powerful destiny ordained*
> *Me some inferior angel, I had stood*
> *Then happy; no unbounded hope had raised*
> *Ambition. Yet why not? Some other Power*
> *As great might have aspired, and me though mean*
> *Drawn to his part; but other Powers as great*
> *Fell not, but stand unshaken, from within*
> *Or from without, to all temptations armed.*
> *Hadst thou the same free will and power to stand?*
> *Thou hadst. Whom hast thou then or what to accuse,*
> *But Heav'n's free love dealt equally to all?*
> *Be then his love accurst, since love or hate,*
> *To me alike, it deals eternal woe.*
> > *(IV, 58–70)*

Satan is remarkably successful in refusing the easier ways out. He counters with what seems to be a motion toward a new beginning based on the full acceptance of personal responsibility:

> *Nay cursed be thou, since against his thy will*
> *Chose freely what it now so justly rues.*
> > *(IV, 71–72)*

At this point he seems close to the George Herbert of "Affliction" (I), who, before he can say the hardest truth, must try out some easier answers:

> *I reade, and sigh, and wish I were a tree;*
> > *For sure then I should grow*
> *To fruit or shade: at least some bird would trust*
> *Her houshold to me, and I should be just.*
>
> *Yet though thou troublest me, I must be meek;*
> > *In weaknesse must be stout.*
> *Well, I will change the service, and go seek*
> > *Some other master out.*
> *Ah my deare God! though I am clean forgot,*
> *Let me not love thee, if I love thee not.*

Or Satan may remind us of the Yeats of "Easter 1916," who wrestles with his deep repugnance toward fanaticism and his personal dislike of certain fanatics he feels compelled to celebrate:

> *What is it but nightfall?*
> *No, no, not night but death;*
> *Was it needless death after all?*
> *For England may keep faith*
> *For all that is done and said.*

But these evasions are no more than the honest effort of one about to testify to a truth he may not understand or love but must acknowledge.[4]

Satan has named the escapes and refused them. As the moment of crisis draws near, his personal grief loses the tone of confession and moves toward despair:

> *Me miserable! which way shall I fly*
> *Infinite wrath, and infinite despair?*
> *Which way I fly is hell; myself am hell;*
>
> . . . .
>
> *O then at last relent: is there no place*
> *Left for repentance, none for pardon left?*
>   *(IV, 73–80)*

The negatives show the way that he is going, and all the minor evasions he has already faced down will be of no help when he reaches the decisive point:

> *None left but by submission; and that word*
> *Disdain forbids me, and my dread of shame*
> *Among the Spirits beneath, whom I seduced*
> *With other promises and other vaunts*
> *Than to submit, boasting I could subdue*
> *Th' Omnipotent.*
>   *(IV, 81–86)*

When he backs away Satan suffers a kind of smaller second fall; unlike the first one it is all acted out in the open. Even as we listen the cosmic pride of the great antagonist turns into familiar channels and fits the patterns of ordinary human pride, not without marks of common vanity.

Just before the crisis a statement of expressive anguish announces the crisis but does not let us know how it will come out; just after, we have a brief lapse into open self-pity:

> Ay me, they little know
> How dearly I abide that boast so vain,
> Under what torments inwardly I groan;
> While they adore me on the throne of hell,
> With diadem and scepter high advanced,
> The lower still I fall, only supreme
> In misery; such joy ambition finds.
>
> (IV, 86–92)

The emotions have their own logic too, and the self-pity is a new confirmation of what has in fact happened. Even the summary statement that severely judges what he has revealed ("such joy ambition finds") manages to sound merely added, an afterthought which cannot affect his inner life. At this low point Satan then discovers a more satisfactory voice and style, one that will serve him often and—though they are unaware of their "imitation"—will serve the Adam and Eve of Boox IX. The style is heightened, as by some undefined exhilaration the source of which we are left to imagine (we may be reminded of that background music which seems to be a technological by-product of the building of Pandemonium); rhetorical reinforcements play and echo with outward confidence; there is room for the momentary concentration of wisdom into apothegm; reasons are as plentiful as blackberries:

> But say I could repent and could obtain
> By act of grace my former state; how soon
> Would highth recall high thoughts, how soon unsay
> What feigned submission swore: ease would recant
> Vows made in pain, as violent and void.
> For never can true reconcilement grow
> Where wounds of deadly hate have pierced so deep;
> Which would but lead me to a worse relapse
> And heavier fall: so should I purchase dear
> Short intermission bought with double smart.
> This knows my Punisher; therefore as far
> From granting he, as I from begging peace.
>
> (IV, 93–104)

The passage glitters and rings, but with the small coins of standard self-deception. It is an impressive display of dramatic rhetoric, but the character and the intelligence both appear diminished. Only toward the end of the speech—when he bids farewell to hope, fear, and remorse, when he gives up good as lost, declaring, "Evil, be thou my good"—does he rise to some of his old magnificence. In most of the passage he is not thinking and feeling through his words; they come forth in brilliant phrasing that seems prearranged, as it were, perhaps to ward off unwelcome thoughts, certainly to reorganize himself at the level of existence he has accepted. In retrospect it seems significant that the idea of submission is not wrestled with, like the idea of gratitude; instead, he says the word "submission" and that is enough: "that word / Disdain forbids me." The central reason enunciated is a negative one backing away, choosing not to choose because of his "dread of shame." If we want a measure of what has happened, we can compare the manipulated ironies of this passage with that earlier note of authentic defiance:

> *Farewell, happy fields,*
> *Where joy for ever dwells! Hail, horrors, hail,*
> *Infernal world, and thou, profoundest hell,*
> *Receive thy new possessor.*
> *(I, 249–52)*

When we next near Satan's voice he has had a full view of Paradise and its human inhabitants. Milton produces a masterly, self-defeating line to sum up the effects: "Scarce thus at length failed speech recovered sad." But recovery comes soon, in the very next line:

> *O hell! what do mine eyes with grief behold!*
> *Into our room of bliss thus high advanced*
> *Creatures of other mold, earth-born perhaps,*
> *Not Spirits, yet to heav'nly Spirits bright*
> *Little inferior; whom my thoughts pursue*
> *With wonder, and could love, so lively shines*
> *In them divine resemblance, and such grace*
> *The hand that formed them on their shape hath*
> *poured.*
> *(IV, 358–65)*

Grief stimulates the general sense of loss, out of which come particular questions that lead to wonder, a state of intellectual elevation that Satan then convincingly expresses. He includes an ambiguous reservation, however, one that seems to mark a barrier between the warmth allowed his language and the warmth that might lead to action. The reservation is "and could love," which sounds as if it might also admit a feeling that could gain ascendance. We shall see two further variations of "could love," and they will remove the ambiguity.

The next stage begins with a strange elegy for the graces of the human pair, but as the strangeness continues the elegiac note becomes harder to recognize:

> *Ah gentle pair, ye little think how nigh*
> *Your change approaches, when all these delights*
> *Will vanish and deliver ye to woe,*
> *More woe, the more your taste is now of joy;*
> *Happy, but for so happy ill secured*
> *Long to continue, and this high seat your heav'n*
> *Ill fenced for Heav'n to keep out such a foe*
> *As now is entered; yet no purposed foe*
> *To you whom I could pity thus forlorn,*
> *Though I unpitied.*
>
> (IV, 366–75)

He seems to be playing a kind of moral shell game as he alternates roles with blurring speed and accompanies himself with some highly distracting rhetorical emphasis—all while he turns "could love" into "could pity" and pauses for a breath of self-pity. Then we get some straight, traditional devil, heavily sardonic:

> *League with you I seek,*
> *And mutual amity so strait, so close,*
> *That I with you must dwell, or you with me*
> *Henceforth; my dwelling haply may not please,*
> *Like this fair Paradise, your sense, yet such*
> *Accept your Maker's work; he gave it me,*
> *Which I as freely give; hell shall unfold,*
> *To entertain you two, her widest gates,*
> *And send forth all her kings; there will be room,*
> *Not like these narrow limits, to receive*
> *Your numerous offspring.*
>
> (IV, 375–85)

When he moves toward his conclusion he can give his feelings greater play. The uncertainties of grief and wonder have been mastered, and he can present his openness to love, which he seems reluctant to renounce, both as testimonial and as sacrifice:

> *if no better place,*
> *Thank him who puts me loth to this revenge*
> *On you who wrong me not, for him who wronged.*
> *And should I at your harmless innocence*
> *Melt, as I do, yet public reason just,*
> *Honor and empire with revenge enlarged*
> *By conquering this new world, compels me now*
> *To do what else though damned I should abhor.*
> *(IV, 385–92)*

Satan draws up into a self-justifying stand, but the rapid, multiple shifts in reference and the acrobatic twists before the final posture comes right—all done with concentrated seriousness—make him flicker like an old film. Satan is the victim of his own comic display, which takes up where the first soliloquy left off. There the inner division was not without some tragic possibilities. Here Satan seems fully aware of what he is doing only when he tries out the role of the hospitable lord of hell. But some kind of awareness, of an undisclosed origin, appears to be operating. For one thing, his response to the intellectual vision of wonder generates less conflict than his earlier response to gratitude. We do not see all of the process, but we can mark the effects. The transfers between thought and feeling now offer little friction or obstacle. Love and pity are isolated for safe expression, and at the end the syntax can even permit a quick embrace of the real thing:

> *And should I at your harmless innocence*
> *Melt, as I do . . . .*

We return to Satan again after he has been listening to the conversation between Adam and Eve. What first moves him to speech is the pain of hell's unfulfilled longing, which is awakened by the sight of the lovers embracing. He begins, therefore, by speaking pure envy. For the first time there is no inner division at all, and Satan seems to have integrated himself at a level that permits him to concentrate on his purpose with minimal distraction. He then continues:

> *Yet let me not forget what I have gained*
> *From their own mouths. All is not theirs, it seems;*
> *One fatal tree there stands, of Knowledge called,*
> *Forbidden them to taste. Knowledge forbidden?*

> *Suspicious, reasonless. Why should their Lord*
> *Envy them that? Can it be sin to know,*
> *Can it be death? And do they only stand*
> *By ignorance, is that their happy state,*
> *The proof of their obedience and their faith?*
> *(IV, 512–20)*

More than one commentator has been persuaded that Satan's questions are just ones. Indeed, to connect ignorance with obedience and faith maligns the Providence the poem wishes to assert, as Milton surely recognized. Even within the speech itself, Milton does not depend only on the pious reader's distrust of Satan, or on the demonstrated ease with which the speaker assigns his own envy to God.

The next words reveal that Satan's questions have been eloquent on two separate levels. First, as the initial response to newly discovered knowledge his questions convey a believable sense of direct immediacy. For the moment there is no expressed feeling of sympathy, but he seems to be identifying himself with Adam and Eve—or at least to be analyzing their circumstances in a manner natural to intellectual sympathy. He is not now persuading himself. But a second level begins to emerge when we recognize that he has been formulating a plan and making a few notes in readiness for the oratory which a favorable occasion may require:

> *O fair foundation laid whereon to build*
> *Their ruin! Hence I will excite their minds*
> *With more desire to know, and to reject*
> *Envious commands, invented with design*
> *To keep them low whom knowledge might exalt*
> *Equal with gods. Aspiring to be such,*
> *They taste and die; what likelier can ensue?*
> *(IV, 521–27)*

He proposes personal efforts to improve his knowledge and does not fail to remind himself that in this business one must be prepared to make the most of all unexpected accidents:

> *But first with narrow search I must walk round*
> *This garden, and no corner leave unspied;*
> *A chance but chance may lead where I may meet*
> *Some wand'ring Spirit of heav'n, by fountain side,*
> *Or in thick shade retired, from him to draw*
> *What further would be learnt.*
> *(IV, 528–33)*

An odd tone creeps in when Satan lingers over the pastoral places where fortunate encouters may be hoped for. "A chance but chance" echoes feebly the sententious defiance on a grand scale studding his early speeches in Book I. Compared even with the desperate rationalizations of the first soliloquy, this sounds nervous, strangely hopeful, and remarkably willing to support conjecture by imagining concrete circumstances. It is a brief, light, comic touch.

There is no inner conflict, but the narrative voice insists on reminding us that the contradictions excluded by the speech have not simply gone away. They reappear in the external appearance of the physical movements:

> *So saying, his proud step he scornful turned,*
> *But with sly circumspection, and began*
> *Through wood, through waste, o'er hill, o'er dale,*
> > *his roam.*
>
> > (IV, 536–38)

Before he leaves, however, Satan formally salutes the lovers, and his language represents internal changes that have occurred since his last soliloquy:

> > *Live while ye may,*
> *Yet happy pair; enjoy, till I return,*
> *Short pleasures, for long woes are to succeed.*
>
> > (IV, 533–35)

The initial pain of longing that grudgingly celebrated the sight of lovers "Imparadised in one another's arms, / The happier Eden," and translated that tormenting spectacle into the terms of personal envy, now presents a terse and brutal translation: the lovers are invited to "enjoy . . . Short pleasures." Though the pity in the earlier speech was corruptible, and though the irony was mannered and sardonic, the expression still was not without some complexity and potential resonance. But when Satan reduces the lovers' paradise to "Short pleasures," the familiar sneering language is directed toward sexual pleasures. The only difference he then needs to admit between hell and paradise is that, for the time being, in paradise "fierce desire" is not "unfulfilled."

We come now to our final, and somewhat different examples, the first of which is not soliloquy but is instead the work of the narrative voice, recreating with summary brilliance the illusion of internal speech. The passage I have in mind follows the explosion of Satan back into his own shape after having been touched by the angelic guard. He answers with impressive scorn the question directed toward his identity: "Not to know me argues yourselves unknown." He sounds like the old Satan—or almost, for though the pride rings out memorably, it is closer to a human pride of position, related to the "dread of shame," than it is to the standards of pride established in Book I. When Zephon replies, "answering scorn with scorn," the effect of his speech on Satan cannot be anticipated by the reader. It is a sharp speech and says many of the right things; what gets under Satan's guard, however, seems to be the moral privilege to say these things rather than any power developed in the expression itself, which is clearly inferior, as art of expression, to Satan's personal brilliance of style. It is the primal virtue of the speaker, as visible Idea, which strikes the memory of Satan and momentarily possesses "the sight of the soul."[5] This is not like the innocence of Adam and Eve, which can be wondered at, almost loved, and almost pitied; some of the feelings previously contained and diverted are now all at once released.

> So spake the Cherub, and his grave rebuke,
> Severe in youthful beauty, added grace
> Invincible. Abashed the Devil stood,
> And felt how awful goodness is, and saw
> Virtue in her shape how lovely; saw, and pined
> His loss; but chiefly to find here observed
> His luster visibly impaired; yet seemed
> Undaunted.
> > (IV, 844–51)

The moment is potentially tragic, as the external view of narrative description strips away the defenses and delivers the internal state of the antagonist to inspection. The first impact is spontaneous, and there is no conflict that Satan can manipulate, part against part, until evil can parlay its derelictions of reason into a position of dominance. He identifies himself with a commanding representation of goodness, and at the same time feels the difference, feels the irrecoverability of the loss. Feeling precedes understanding, but the case is not, like that of gratitude, one in which an ambiguous feeling can be handled by complex exchanges, during which what was forgotten is remembered, struggled with, understood, accepted, and then quietly diverted by its being forgotten again. Nor do we have, as in the case of wonder, an understanding expressed with feeling but carefully held in check by the reservation "could love."

Part of what Milton accomplishes by this enclosed moment is a valuable imaginative surprise. An internal action demonstrates the effectiveness of those laws governing the intellectual and spiritual diminution of evil, its loss of the capacity to do good, and yet its fixed, unseverable attachment to good. A character whose progressive degeneration has been voluntary, who has been fulfilling the laws on schedule, so to speak, under their control but acting as if on his own initiative, with every step revealing both his own immediate motives and the governing perspective—suddenly that character seems to reverse the established progress and its rhythm. He succumbs wholly to what he has been opposing. The moral laws—and their attendant traditions of commentary prepared to anticipate all such exigencies—are not disturbed by the suddenness and spontaneity; all of the surprise falls upon the reader's expectations, his human sympathies, his generous response to the strange currents of tragedy, and falls upon his recognition, a moment later, that all is really as it was. Two further stages recover the established rhythm of Satan's progress. The first shock (the "felt," "saw," "pined") is translated into the common pride of "dread of shame," as we are told that he is "chiefly" grieved by the hostile, objective report on his appearance. We are told this in a completely neutral voice, as if the fact were self-explanatory and were not part of a process deserving scrutiny and comment. The first immediacy of grief was altogether too intense and convincing to be dissipated by so easy a transfer. Satan needs to believe that the minor reason of nettled pride is the chief cause of that sudden shock, and to believe this with a swift, unacknowledged *fiat* which emulates spontaneity; otherwise, he may have to retrace his path to the crossroads where the choice of repentance may have to be faced again. Finally, at the third stage, whatever the visible damage to his "luster," his external appearance tightly covers the released agonies felt: "yet seemed / Undaunted."

For this complex moment, which interrupts the established progress and imposes a retrospective movement, Milton prefers to employ the narrative voice, by means of which he can at the same time simulate internal monologue and retain the flexible controls of an external view. In Book IX, when the internal conflict does not have much left to show,

Milton again chooses the narrative voice for the moment of greatest intensity, Satan's first approach to Eve, which separates him from his evil and leaves him "abstracted," "Stupidly good." But the closest parallel with the episode we have been examining is that moment in hell when Satan gets ready for the first public address to the fallen host. Here too the narrative voice, besides furnishing tears and sighs, commands a retrospective movement and simulates a monologue of the mind:

> Cruel his eye, but cast
> Signs of remorse and passion to behold
> The fellows of his crime, the followers rather
> (Far other once beheld in bliss), condemned
> For ever now to have their lot in pain,
> Millions of Spirits for his fault amerced
> Of heav'n, and from eternal splendors flung
> For his revolt, yet faithful how they stood,
> Their glory withered . . . .
>
> (I, 604–12)

With Book V Satan disappears from the time present of the poem and returns, to take advantage of what is at last ready in Book IX. There are two soliloquies, his last, and both are disappointing performances, of the sort any good writer must be willing to provide when his character is groping in a genuine trough. The conflict within him has nothing new to show us, and he can only repeat, with appropriately fainter and looser expressions, what we have already seen. The enormous creative energy that Satan evokes from Milton does not lessen; it simply moves away from the exhausted center of Satan's own expression of his inner life. The voice of the narrator quickens and, in the extended simile beginning "As one who long in populous city pent," renews our interest in the force of Satan's response to innocence. Another burst of energy describes the serpent's approach to Eve:

> Circular base of rising folds, that tow'red
> Fold above fold a surging maze; his head
> Crested aloft, and carbuncle his eyes;
> With burnished neck of verdant gold, erect
> Amidst his circling spires, that on the grass
> Floated redundant.
>
> (IX, 498–503)

Nor does he advance alone, without the accompaniment of famous future serpents and other comparison:

> *As when a ship by skilful steersman wrought*
> *Nigh river's mouth or foreland, where the wind*
> *Veers oft, as oft so steers, and shifts her sail.*
>   *(IX, 513–15)*

The greatest energy, of course, goes into Satan's role as a master of disguise acting as a philanthropical orator.

That the first soliloquy in Book IV and the first in Book IX are almost of a length helps underscore their differences. The Satan who slips back into Paradise in a mist and plans to work through the serpent pours out his grief and "bursting passion into plaints," but everything is diluted. Some of the self-deceptions, now that they no longer involve live issues and might be believed by the speaker, begin to sound like clichés vitalized by jokes. His wittiest effort, though entertaining, depends on a flimsy pose and verbal turns:

> *To me shall be the glory sole among*
> *The infernal Powers, in one day to have marred*
> *What he, Almighty styled, six nights and days*
> *Continued making, and who knows how long*
> *Before had been contriving!*
> . . . .
>   *He to be avenged,*
> *And to repair his numbers thus impaired,*
> *Whether such virtue spent of old now failed*
> *More angels to create, if they at least*
> *Are his created, or to spite us more . . . .*
>   *(IX, 135–47)*

The rest of the speech is a wandering variety of praise, complaint, self-pity, confession, and sonorously empty moral pronouncement. There is no conflict and no hurry; he moves through matters that have become routine. If we are surprised at all, it is that he still has to keep on making these verbal motions, and at such length.

In the last soliloquy before approaching Eve he recites again his lesson that destruction is his only joy and grieves again over the weakness he feels, "to what I was in heav'n." There is a momentary flutter of still unextinguished response to beauty and love, but the last word is the voluntary one, hate, "under show of love well feigned." The indignity he voices—

> *now constrained*
> *Into a beast, and mixed with bestial slime,*
> *This essence to incarnate and imbrute. . . .*
> *(IX, 164–66)*

—is an empty verbalism and a tired lapse of memory compared with the genuine ache of confinement produced by the narrative voice that describes his entrance into the serpent:

> *In at his mouth*
> *The Devil entered, and his brutal sense,*
> *In heart or head, possessing soon inspired*
> *With act intelligential, but his sleep*
> *Disturbed not, waiting close th' approach of morn.*
> *(IX, 187–91)*

The "waiting close" which Keats justly admired, sums up the constrictions of Satan's inner state, and does so by drawing on the art of the narrative voice to intensify chosen external details while recreating the inside of events.

Having transformed intellectual pride into "dread of shame" and hatred of God into personal envy, he turns with practiced ease the despairing of revenge into the expression of spite, first attributing God's creation of "this man of clay" to divine spite. He is forced to use and pervert reason, but to do without it, as to revoke his creation, lies beyond his power. (Adam, we shall see, can go beyond Satan's limits at the crucial moment.) Satan can manage the "show of love well feigned," but even his hatred partly fails him and is diminished, like the evil he nominates as his "good." The master of disguise has talked himself around and under all the inner obstructions of his native endowment, and in drawing his personal map has pioneered the classical routes.

Until the human fall occurs, nothing in Satan's experience fully coincides with the speech, actions, or inner life of Adam and Eve. There are, nevertheless, multiple *coincidences,* in the secondary sense, many circumstantial approximations suggesting relationship. Satan is a reflector who invokes or is the occasion for echoes and premonitions,

> *Of calling shapes, and beck'ning shadows dire,*
> *And airy tongues that syllable men's names.*[6]

The similar is not, however, the same. The relationships exercise our attention, increase our interest in the story, challenge our capacity to discriminate, and challenge our natural ambivalence toward anticipating and not anticipating the promised certainty of disastrous events. The relationships are not causal; they are the reflections of a traumatized oracle expressing perplexed truth. The foreknowledge expressed always needs sorting out and is a comment, not an influence, on events, for the matter of relationship is always our, the readers', problem. Adam and Eve are unaware of Satan's personal revelation. What they learn by report concerns only the outline of his public career. They are equally unaware of the public revelation that takes place before the throne of God in Book III. This, the background of true foreknowledge, of announced failure, and of the new joy revealed, that of love as sacrifice, which will turn failure into salvation, is also part of the readers' knowledge as we respond to the story while we sift the silences and the significance in analogies that bear upon but do not touch the free actions at the center.

IV.

The Story at the Center

If I foreknew,
Foreknowledge had no influence on their fault,
Which had no less proved certain unforeknown.
So without least impulse or shadow of fate,
Or aught by me immutably foreseen,
They trespass, authors to themselves in all . . . .
(III, 117–22)

Those are hard words, set forth in the unique language of omniscience, which must also comprehend the various shapes of muttering the pronouncement will evoke. The sentence may not confuse an audience of angelic listeners, fit and not few, though fewer than they were. But even that audience will receive, through the dialogue undertaken by the Son of God, a kind of seminar short-course of instruction for understanding the style of omniscience, which is not likely, if there is an authorized concordance in heaven, to have many entries under *if*—"If I foreknew." A human audience, at least a seventeenth-century one, will have certain educational advantages to compensate for the distance from the source and center of learning: that audience will possess the multiple translations provided by the willing industry of theologians and then "delivered plainly in way of precepts, or sermoned at large." Or the translation may come from another kind of well-head, and by another method, which Spenser called "doctrine by ensample" rather than by rule, and Sidney went out of his way to call by the simplest name possible, "a tale."[1]

This is the first of my assumptions for the discourse which is to follow: that Milton is telling a story. It is an old story, well known and well pondered, which does not preclude suspense but does make surprise difficult and dangerous. A simple story, it staggers under the weight of significance retrospectively applied—by individuals, by schools, and by armies of exegetes. An ambitious narrative artist will face major obstacles. To begin with, he must honor the tale by telling it freshly, as if for the first time, so that it lives and works in the reader's mind, but does not over-stimulate him with novelties which may irritate him to resist or question. At the same time the fictional assumption that this is the first telling of the story must accept certain understood obligations. The privilege and the burden cannot escape their intimate relatedness. As an authentic beginning of human experience, as a story invested with authority, the account must ring true; for its reverberations will be heard by ears trained in a long tradition of reasoned interpretations, and will be felt by hearts deeply influenced by individual and collective dreamwork. The story must *typify*, must anticipate and answer the expectations concerning an unfallen Adam and Eve who represent man and woman before the loss of innocence, and who reveal essential human character in the very shape of the catastrophe. The habits of mind formed by typological traditions made it normal to read Scripture as a system of cross-references and anticipations foreshadowing the advent of Christ. By extension, such reading sought insight into other crises in the life of man and in the revelations of God's will, and the emphasis of Protestant theology tended to give typological thinking further retrospective and reciprocal dimensions, by which contemporary spiritual experience could be understood in the light of scriptural events. The first story therefore anticipated every present time, and if the many ways in which it did so were obvious and were made dull by repetition, the story itself was too important in its consequences and too mysterious in its parabolic brevities to be worn out by the cataloguings and applications to which it was subjected. Every detail—and the implied pauses, timing, and silences—might reasonably fascinate and yield a valuable clue to the understanding of man by man.

Milton and his first qualified readers would have understood and accepted these and other conditions. In engaging himself to "justify the ways of God to men" Milton has implicitly accepted the humanist goal of justifying man's ways to men. The action he presents, if it is to be worthy of his "great argument," must answer in reasonable ways all the uncertainties which reasonable Christians have named or felt in the story of the first human crisis. The literal and philosophical truths of the story may not be coaxed into positions that, however exciting or attractive, will seem eccentric or witty, and the responsible freedom to develop and elaborate where Scripture is silent or brief must nevertheless avoid seeming to improve on the story by telling beautiful lies. At the very least the poet must lie properly, as Homer taught, but the nature of his obligation to his material is more demanding. His first invocation proclaims a soaring confidence in the materials and a humble faith in the divine support necessary for the poetic task. He never mentions but everywhere shows a comprehensive awareness of the scrupulous tact which he must exert on his own initiative—making the numerous choices that will find him to be a poet made as well as born, and by "merit" equal to the poetic undertaking.

There are besides many technical difficulties which the poet must solve for himself with minimal assistance from the Muse. The traditional guides of literary verisimilitude cannot be followed but must, as it were, be reinvented for a story without human precedent. As for problems of background and foreground, they are so constant in the poem—and in the deep truth of the story, its exemplary force and subsequent history of interpretation—that they may seem to have a part in every serious critical question. To some extent Milton's problems are those of any poet telling a known story and having to work out individual ways of creating suspense along the measured approaches to the inevitable. The artist's genius in discovering the one right way to tell a story—like other great discoveries will seem astonishingly simple and absolute in retrospect. We cannot clearly distinguish between his capacity to analyze the general and particular difficulties of the narrative conditions and his capacity to solve those difficulties. It seems easier to attribute a more decisive role to inspiration in the solving of problems than in their analysis, but this may well be a sentimental predisposition of the critical mind, which seldom finds itself inspired in the performance of basic tasks and prefers to attend the author's dazzling successes, which we all love and find inspiring. Somewhere in his preparations, nevertheless, before the verse began to be "easy" and "unpremeditated," Milton had to reach a decision that could not possibly be trusted to impromptu tactics. He needed to invent and sustain an intricate balance capable of expressing, without normal methods of narrative continuity and development, the singular movement from *the* original innocence to *the* first disobedience. God's hard words on foreknowledge are the established rules of the story, and the poet's borrowed omniscience must justify itself by creating Adam and Eve "Sufficient . . . though free . . . authors to themselves in all."

A second assumption is the one I have just now touched on. The balance that is Milton's technical device for managing the story is also, I believe, a deep and pervasive figure through which he can express the involved relations of love on earth and the grander simplicity of love in heaven. The last assumption that I wish to bring forward is this: what happens in heaven must of necessity provide the perfect pattern for what should happen on earth. Milton does not neglect his obligations, but neither does he force what is unprecedented in the human experience to conform at every point with the divine model. Here I must undertake a brief argument to clear some ground for the story.

Milton develops the world of human love so that in some ways, like the bower of Adam and Eve and their "genial bed," it stands a little apart, even from the great universal models to which it is nevertheless answerable. The supreme model is the creative action of God's love, most fully expressed by Milton's beautiful account of the creation of the world—an account that harmonizes theology and esthetics by a poetic distillation of a familiar Christian argument for the existence of God, the so-called argument from design, from the beauty and order of the existent world. Such divine love does not offer a pattern that can be imitated, but rather imposes imperatives and demonstrates the grounds for human response. The highest imitable example in heaven is provided by God's Son, who volunteers to sacrifice his own existence by descending to atone for man. That example defines concepts and standards by which we can measure the actions of Adam and Eve. But the Son's example occurs in heavenly time, which is not fully synchronized with human time. Not until Book IX is there any occasion that would make sacrifice and denial of self a model for direct human imitation. In other words, Milton has transposed a significant moment of God's time into a conceptual mode that may be contemplated by the reader as he witnesses the two kinds of time approach and cross each other. But the actors cannot know what happened in heaven. For them, though not for the reader, when the precise future moment arrives, the Son's example of divine love, knowledge, and freedom would require an apprehension more intuitive than discursive. At the time of the fall the imitation is parody: Eve declares that she did it all for Adam, and Adam is willing to sacrifice his own life—not *for* her but to remain united with her.

In the pause between the Son's offer and the Father's acceptance the narrator's description fixes the simultaneous movements downward and upward in an equilibrium which has great authority as an expression of divine order:

> *His words here ended, but his meek aspect*
> *Silent yet spake, and breathed immortal love*
> *To mortal men, above which only shone*
> *Filial obedience.*
>
> (*III, 266–69*)

Here the proceeding from and returning to God are not part of a process (as in Raphael's exposition to Adam) but exist as a simultaneity, timeless but applicable to all moments of human love. With minor modification the balance defines Adam's authorized love for Eve while he stands at the same time "for God only." If the equilibrium exerts less hold on Eve, who has no children yet but only flowers upon which to expend the creative energy of love's downward motion, that is a problem Milton had to accept with his story, and he must do with it what he can.

In Book VII, just before the angelic account of the masterwork of creation, man's nature is defined in terms of upward and downward motion. Man is

> *self-knowing, and from thence*
> *Magnanimous to correspond with heav'n,*
> *But grateful to acknowledge whence his good*
> *Descends.*
>
> (*VII, 510–13*)

This pattern also carries great authority in the poem, but human knowledge, one must conclude, is not represented by an equilibrium as simple as that demonstrated by the Son. The expression of return comes first, the immediate motion upward derived from self-knowledge. Then the motion downward is recorded, the good that derives from God, which produces the moral virtue of gratitude, which returns to the source in acknowledgement. So God's one movement downward is balanced against two ascending movements, one expressed by the lofty virtue of magnanimity, which corresponds, the other by humble gratitude, which responds. This pattern allows for the movements of human time, for the immediacy of self-knowledge and the different rhythm of acknowledgement, which is more protracted and involves the inwardness of feeling.

The conceptual form of the divine order expresses itself in vertical structures; what is new in the relations of Adam and Eve is the introduction of a sense of movement on the horizontal plane. As Adam's equilibrium in self-knowledge and acknowledgement is more complex than the shining simplicity of the Son's equilibrium in love and obedience, so we have an increasing complexity with the introduction of Eve, a complexity of balancing the horizontal human movements between *two* people while keeping these movements in proper balance with the vertical movements that proceed from and return to God. Milton must have expected his fit readers to recognize the potential opportunities for stress and imbalance. One of the apparent attributes of Milton's God is that He creates dialectical opportunities for "filial freedom" to express itself in *receiving* the divine intentions. And so we may witness the cosmic "novelty on earth" of two creatures forgiving each other. On the other hand, we may mark limits and differences. Adam's "active sphere assigned" is the uncharted one of human love, which must reflect the highest value of "filial obedience," but he cannot in the same way, without some intervening translation, be expected to show immortal love for mortal woman.

I now leave these abstruse matters and turn to the pleasures of the story. Definition begins where it should, with our first view of the human pair. Their appearance, initially dignified to the point of stiffness, neglects all ordinary rules of description. They are declared to be in accord with the reality they represent and from which they are derived. We are required to see them with the mind's eye, registering the abstract qualities of ontological truth. The syntax, with its insistent linkings and repetitions, is a kind of idiomatic image that also expresses the dominant sense of derivation. The next lines begin to emphasize their differences, in sex, function, and purpose, moving toward a separate but highly selective description of each person, and finally to a full statement of their intimate and reciprocal relations:

> His fair large front and eye sublime declared
> Absolute rule; and hyacinthine locks
> Round from his parted forelock manly hung
> Clust'ring, but not beneath his shoulders broad:
> She as a veil down to the slender waist
> Her unadorned golden tresses wore
> Disheveled, but in wanton ringlets waved
> As the vine curls her tendrils, which implied
> Subjection, but required with gentle sway,
> And by her yielded, by him best received,
> Yielded with coy submission, modest pride,
> And sweet reluctant amorous delay.
> (IV, 300–11)

Though Adam is the dominant partner, the description of Eve is more intricate, intense, and detailed. However muted, here is a firm admonition of Eve's human right and dignity in the *gentleness* that is required of Adam. Her yielding lies within her own will, and his primary powers of contemplation and valor must accept a humble domestic range of allowable expression: "by him best received." So there are two significant limitations placed upon Adam's "absolute rule." A third of the poem will go by before Adam confides to Raphael an important range of his inner feelings toward Eve. But we cannot mistake the initial implications: though man has true authority and absolute rule, the laws of human love require some new proceedings, in which the masculine rule in love is to receive, a rule which is not pronounced absolute or established by argument, but simply and unequivocally called "best." Furthermore, the limitations assigned Adam are characterized by simple restraints, but Eve's emotional life is presented as working through inner conflicts which directly concern Adam though all of the description centers on her:

> Yielded with coy submission, modest pride,
> And sweet reluctant amorous delay.
> (IV, 310–11)

A hundred lines later we hear the voices of Adam and Eve as they introduce themselves in their first speech that the poem records. If we compare the dignity and power of what is, chronologically, Adam's first speech—his account of how his life began, described to Raphael in Book VIII—we may observe that in Book IV Milton is taking fictional advantage of the illusion of newness to allow Adam some innocent awkwardness which is not quite in accord with his figure drawn to the mind's eye. Commenting on the fact that the tree of life is planted by the tree of knowledge, Adam says to Eve:

> *So near grows death to life, whate'er death is,*
> *Some dreadful thing no doubt; for well thou know'st . . . .*
>
> *(IV, 425–26)*

Milton's tact prevents the lines from standing out in the context, but they can be heard, and they are not a satisfying expression of either domestic authority or the divine gift of contemplation. The reader who has just heard the verbal acrobatics of Satan in soliloquy may for a moment doubt his ears when Adam says:

> *Then let us not think hard*
> *One easy prohibition, who enjoy*
> *Free leave so large to all things else.*
>
> *(IV, 432–34)*

One remembers not only Satan's display but God's pronouncement that man will "easily transgress the sole command."

Adam's lecture is a preface to the main episode, Eve's narrative account of her experiences upon first awakening into life. Adam will tell his own story, much later, to Raphael. Both the differences and the similarities are finely drawn.[2] For instance, Eve's first questions on existence resemble Adam's, but his questions arise after twenty lines of significant activity, much of it turned outward, and once his questions are expressed they are followed to their conclusion. Eve begins by wondering about the "who" and "where." Adam's "from what cause" no doubt has a proper philosophical ring; Eve is more concrete and matter of fact: "whence hither brought." She wonders but not long, for she is distracted by the "murmuring sound" of water and then by the image of herself. Adam's monologue was answered by the voice of God: "called by thee I come." Eve needed the intervention of a warning voice to lead her from herself to Adam.

Her obedience to the voice is prompt and would go unmarked if Eve did not call attention to her awareness that she was obeying:

> *What could I do*
> *But follow straight, invisibly thus led?*
> *(IV, 475–76)*

The end of this episode presents Adam speaking as a lover, pleading with Eve as she turns back toward the more attractive image in the pool:

> *Return, fair Eve,*
> *Whom fli'st thou? Whom thou fli'st, of him thou art,*
> *His flesh, his bone; to give thee being I lent*
> *Out of my side to thee, nearest my heart,*
> *Substantial life, to have thee by my side*
> *Henceforth an individual solace dear.*
> *Part of my soul I seek thee, and thee claim*
> *My other half.*
> *(IV, 481–88)*

I pause here at the end of Adam's quoted speech and will return to Eve's final words.

The accents are those of human love. There can be no such language in heaven, as there are no materials of flesh and bone, no conceptual metaphors of divided souls, no anxious feelings of separation and loss. It is a passionate speech, something new in the world. One has no reason to distrust the simple directness of what Adam says or to compare it unfavorably with the language of love in heaven. And if one compares Eve's account with Adam's version of the scene as he later relates it to Raphael, the differences do not seem especially important. There are some minor alterations and omissions not inappropriate to the new context. That Adam suppresses the dominance of his own role may be the allowed modesty of a story told in the first person, and there are no clear signals prompting us to question his motives. But in retrospect a moment later, when he reveals the discovery of passion, we may perhaps have some second thoughts. (Milton has many ways of keeping the problems of love in sight and motion, with opposing tendencies held suspended until the last possible instant.) In the account to Raphael, Eve's approval is the main point, her yielding and his receiving. The standards of "pleaded reason" are not exactly those of other prominent examples—Adam's first dialogue with his Creator, the Son's pleaded reason to the Father, or the crucial dialogue in Book IX where Adam's pleaded reason fails to dissuade Eve from turning away. We can hardly be unaware of these parallels, but they do not lend themselves to any simple pointing of a moral, unless that indeed is the moral.

To return to Eve's story and one strange effect of Adam's words. Eve is repeating the speech to Adam, presenting him with an auditory image of himself as the eloquent, successful lover. Most of Adam's children, I believe, like to be quoted with approval. That Adam is flattered by the speaking image of himself is obvious. A moment later he is embracing her and smiling

> *with superior love, as Jupiter*
> *On Juno smiles, when he impregns the clouds*
> *That shed May flowers.*
> *(IV, 499–501)*

The allusion, drawn out as a decorative myth, makes a fine flourish that carries our attention away from the risks of "superior love." At this point the Devil takes over "with jealous leer malign" and produces an intense, fascinating soliloquy. (Here, as in hundreds of places, the mastery of timing and tempo seems effortless and is absolute.)

The satisfaction of Narcissus requires only a simple reflecting surface. Eve provides a complex reflection; she is beautiful and loved, and she is reproducing for the recognition of her admiring audience, no doubt with grace and evident pleasure, the winning words that she has memorized. This is the complex narcissism of courtship carried into wedded love, but if reason is choice on a humble plane too, then no rational being would prefer the solitary, limited joys available to Narcissus. As Eve speaks and acts out Adam's image, she is also consciously the person whose approval is sought by that "pleaded reason." Her words can evoke the "answering looks / Of sympathy and love," to be found in her listener no less than in the reflecting pool, for the spoken words now create an audible image of herself more satisfying than eyes alone could discover. It is an image that she did not know about, and it pleases her, as it should.

God, having spoken once and temporarily ruled her will,

turns over to Adam the task of free persuasion, and Eve's final words (which I omitted from the previous quotation) will testify that Adam has been successful:

> *With that thy gentle hand*
> *Seized mine, I yielded, and from that time see*
> *How beauty is excelled by manly grace*
> *And wisdom, which alone is truly fair.*
> *(IV, 488–91)*

Her acknowledgement is the right one to make, her willingness now to be visibly led. In reaffirming values established elsewhere in the poem, Eve is expressing her own free pledge of magnanimous correspondence with the God in Adam, and she has dropped her charming role in a love play to speak in her own character. If Adam is flattered by this lofty image of himself, it is nevertheless not one that he can enjoy passively. If his love cannot be encompassed by his gratitude, then Adam's wisdom—in her eyes too—may be "discountenanced." This is the point of Raphael's later warning that Eve's beauty was intended not only to delight Adam but to bind him to his "other self" in honor and awe:

> *So awful, that with honor thou may'st love*
> *Thy mate, who sees when thou art seen least wise.*
> *(VIII, 577–78)*

For the mysterious power of beauty transforms a flattering image into a psychological imperative, and Adam will be held by the need to appear "truly fair" in his wife's eyes.

Eve's acknowledgement of "manly grace" and "wisdom" may be read, I think, without trying to gauge the presence of narrative reservation or irony. The potential strain in her continuing to see Adam in this light does not need to be emphasized. It is present in the fable as Milton develops it, and only a resolute or naive reader will be immune to all vibrations. For instance, her first speech, in response to Adam's introductory lecture, seems to anticipate her praise of wisdom, but with a suggestive uncertainty in the tone of personal feeling:

> *what thou hast said is just and right.*
> *For we to him indeed all praises owe,*
> *And daily thanks, I chiefly who enjoy*
> *So far the happier lot, enjoying thee.*
> *(IV, 443–46)*

She is still learning the language of intellectual acquiescence, echoing her husband, and the intensity of her personal desire for wisdom will be revealed in due time. But we should not miss the contrast between the passionate force of Adam's love speech and her own measured expressions of intellectual obedience.

Within its narrative and dramatic leisure, then, the introduction of Adam and Eve presents in brief many of the materials of potential conflict. Satan and his soliloquies indicate one external source of pressure leading to destructive action. The dialogue in heaven has imposed another external pressure, that of a supreme example of creative action—the Son voicing the Father's intention and expressing an auditory image of the beatific vision. Milton has a long story to tell, and the conditions of that story require that he avoid many of the usual devices for developing sequential action. He clearly presents but limits those predispositions and tendencies which must not be treated as causes that lead to inevitable effects. Once the fall occurs, however, Milton is free to compensate for the systematic development hitherto denied him, and he is grimly methodical in exhibiting every step in the consequences of sin. But until the fall he must produce and draw out a new and difficult kind of dramatic narrative, one that presents episodes which are suggestive but not fully developed, which are deliberately parallel but are not identical and are left without formal connections.

As the reader's view of the first day in Paradise draws to an end, Eve presents a love song to Adam:

> *With thee conversing I forget all time,*
> *All seasons and their change, all please alike.*
> *Sweet is the breath of morn, her rising sweet,*
> *With charm of earliest birds; pleasant the sun*
> *When first on this delightful land he spreads*
> *His orient beams, on herb, tree, fruit, and flow'r,*
> *Glist'ring with dew; fragrant the fertile earth*
> *After soft showers; and sweet the coming on*
> *Of grateful ev'ning mild, then silent night*
> *With this her solemn bird and this fair moon,*
> *And these the gems of heav'n, her starry train:*
> *But neither breath of morn when she ascends*
> *With charm of earliest birds, nor rising sun*
> *On this delightful land, nor herb, fruit, flow'r,*

Glist'ring with dew, nor fragrance after showers,
Nor grateful ev'ning mild, nor silent night
With this her solemn bird, nor walk by moon
Or glittering starlight without thee is sweet.
                                        (IV, 639–56)

Eve's love speech, though "unmeditated," is a poem, highly cultivated in its grace of expression. Her declaration of love is in style and content, as in circumstances, entirely different from the example of Adam's "pleaded reason" which we have heard. Yet her starting point is an echo of Adam's earlier statement that their gardening task is "delightful," and even "were it toilsome, yet with thee were sweet." The general effect is to present Adam with another speaking image of himself—not by quoting his words on this occasion, but by composing variations on a borrowed theme in order to praise him as the only begetter of this poem.

Within this general effect we may observe two interesting complications. Eve's poem distantly resembles the angelic hymn in Book III which celebrated the Son's "unexampled love" for man, but in that hymn the movement keeps renewing its forward energy by naming and returning to the subject of praise, "thee." Eve's poem revolves around Adam, begins with him and at the end gracefully delivers all the intervening perceptions that she has composed for him. Her love song is generally admired. Does the lack of Adam's presence in the poem raise any open or subliminal question? It may be heavy-handed to ask whether Adam's absence from the body of the poem anticipates his abrupt disappearance from Eve's account of her dream, or his prominent absence from Eve's consciousness during Satan's temptation, to return only after she has eaten the forbidden fruit. On the other hand, the reader who has observed these parallels cannot be expected to annihilate them from his awareness. We are left, I believe, where Milton intended us to be—supporting still another question that we can formulate out of the craft of experience but cannot answer. Indeed, the way the story is conducted we are obliged to challenge the validity of a question that the formal arrangement of the story allows, and perhaps invites, us to recognize.

The second complication I have in mind is this: the poem is for Adam but it is about Eve. She is the creative center, perceiving objects and movements, naming and arranging them with conscious artistic delight. A poem of this kind has to be centered in the self, the stimulated source of individual creative perception. Once Eve has chosen the form of her poem, or made her first "unmeditated" step, then she must perceive through her own concentrated senses if she is to offer a true poem to Adam. There is no way to examine or judge her act of choice. We may say, if we wish to exercise our knowledge of things human, that what is precarious or ambiguous in the balance between her subjective experience and her objective purpose has recognizable analogues, and indeed constitutes an established artistic and human dilemma. We may also say, with no less assurance, that Milton's act of choice fits his own artistic purpose, and very well.[3]

Our next scene, the last we shall consider in the first stage of the story, is Milton's daring inclusion of a familiar domestic episode in the ideal life of the garden.[4] A heavenly guest arrives at meal time and puts the new household into a state of some excitement. Eve is busy inside preparing the noon meal while Adam rests in the shady doorway waiting. The sight of the angel startles Adam, and he calls out abruptly, dropping the formal address which is the custom in Paradise: "Haste hither, Eve, and worth thy sight behold." Adam hopes that the angel brings them an important message and will be their guest. By the time he has decided this, Eve's leisure for beholding has come to an end. He says:

> But go with speed,
> And what thy stores contain, bring forth and pour
> Abundance, fit to honor and receive
> Our heav'nly stranger; well we may afford
> Our givers their own gifts, and large bestow
> From large bestowed, where Nature multiplies
> Her fertile growth, and by disburd'ning grows
> More fruitful; which instruct us not to spare.
> *(V, 313–20)*

It is an awkward speech and overarticulated. No doubt the unexpected social situation produces a measure of anxiety even in Paradise. Adam's characteristic response is to exercise his chief virtue, his wisdom, with more than a little solemnity of gesture and phrasing. If he is nervous about the angel, at least he can explain the nature of things to Eve. But he is also acting in a way that is but lightly protected from our view of things. He is instructing his wife in her own business, the kitchen affairs, and is setting a precedent that can be depended upon to elicit the same response from unfallen as from fallen woman.[5] Eve replies with a delicate touch of impatience, lavishing a careful formality of address upon him, turning her own solemn phrases, and matching his own display of wisdom with her own, not without a suggestion of deliberate pedanticism:

> Adam, earth's hallowed mold,
> Of God inspired, small store will serve, where store,
> All seasons, ripe for use hangs on the stalk;
> Save what by frugal storing firmness gains
> To nourish, and superfluous moist consumes.
> (V, 321–25)

The tensions of domestic love are perhaps not quite covered by the laws of "gentle sway" and yielding and receiving. If I am right in detecting a suggestion of parody in Eve's reply, then Adam is now hearing an image of himself that he has not heard before. But again it is a brief moment, undeveloped, and submerged in the flow of new action. Eve directs herself to her task as hostess, accepts the need for haste, and begins planning her menu. And so she goes out into the mid-day sun, "more warmth than Adam needs," obeying with no argument but only a few comments a husband who for the first time seems chiefly concerned with himself and with matters that relegate her to a peripheral position. We can see the domestic tensions, though they are slight, and for a moment we see the lovers thinking and feeling separately about the same situation, one that emphasizes the difference in their roles. Adam is now dividing their domestic duties, sending Eve away to work separately at what she does best while he goes forth to welcome the "heav'nly stranger." The episode is hardly a rehearsal for what is to happen in Book IX, but, given the necessary restraints of Milton's narrative, the scene is a daring invention, one that reveals latent possibilities while not permitting them to assume a definite shape.

In permitting us to glimpse Adam and Eve, not as lovers, and less as ideal husband and wife than as man and woman, Milton touches with delicate discrimination upon a difference between them. We have just heard Adam's "manly grace" of wisdom take a turn that suggests the pompous, and

we think that Eve, though innocent, may have heard something that resembles what we hear. To his "and large
bestow / From large bestowed" she offers a revised echo:

> *small store will serve, where store,*
> *All seasons, ripe for use hangs on the stalk;*
> *Save what by frugal storing . . . .*

Her particular concrete knowledge is different from his, and
she makes a display of it, but she also expresses a deeper
difference of her feminine nature. Surprised by an unexpected
event, Adam's magnanimity to correspond with heaven
sounds less than admirable; so too his gratitude: "well we
may afford / Our givers their own gifts." Eve's version gives
the gratitude a mild competitive tendency. She will entertain
the angel so well that he

> *Beholding shall confess that here on earth*
> *God hath dispensed his bounties as in heav'n.*
> *(V, 329–30)*

We are probably invited to smile, but not to blame the hostess, or the woman. The masculine and feminine flaws here
touched on are minor, and insignificant if temporary. But
they do go in different directions. By the end of the poem the
tendencies we see here will be thoroughly drilled out of
Adam. But Milton will allow Eve to keep her humanizing
weakness as a kind of "modest pride," a necessary support for
hope. Her last words in the poem will recall the attitude she is
expressing now.

Let us pause to bring in other matters. The narrative line
which dominates the center of Book IV breaks in Book V, or
rather begins a sweeping curve when Raphael moves away
from matters of direct concern to Adam and Eve to narrate
matters which concern them, but indirectly, by reflection.
Raphael turns from his lecture on the scale of being to the
story of the war in heaven, and concludes by making the
explicit connection: the "terrible example" of Satan "Who
now is plotting how he may seduce / Thee also from obedience." The narrative voice repeats and extends the lesson,
and then Adam asks for and is told the story of the creation.
Except for Raphael's brief, significant comments before and
after the creation of man, all of the lesson is indirect—
implicit in the example of God's love, the beauty of the

world, and man's position. In Book VIII the movement begins to return to the center, first with the dialogue on astronomy, which Adam initiates. The lesson is entirely different now, as Adam tries to "scan" the secrets of the universe and is treated by the angel to an exhibition of "quaint opinions wide" which later conjecture will produce. At this point we do not have solid, objective examples like Satan, Abdiel, and the Son, or indirect examples which reason may be expected to translate in one simple motion. Instead, the example concerns for the first time an isolated exhibition of Adam's mind in doubt, puzzling over "studious thoughts abstruse." The form of dialogue, the angelic humor, and the intimations of emerging human nature anticipate Adam's dialogue with God and the exchanges (without overt humor) on the subject of sex, on earth as it is and is not in heaven. Under his mild jesting Raphael presents an unambiguous reminder that the life in Paradise has its own due range of intellectual obligation and privilege not to be diverted into dreaming of other worlds. Adam responds and develops the angel's brief lecture with one of his own, demonstrating that he has understood the issue and that he is a prompt, alert participant in dialogue.

What may be considered the second stage of the human story begins toward the end of the first systematic and sustained account of human life from the beginning to the narrative present. Adam reviews, fills in details, amplifies, and adds substantial material we did not know before. The length (three hundred lines, nearly half of Book VIII) and the continuity from a single perspective mark a change in the pace of Milton's narrative, as Adam's story, in spite of its continuity, moves across the transition between the first and second stages of the human drama. Though most of the episode is unhurried, it ends with Adam's unexpected disclosure of passion in the last forty lines of his story, an abrupt novelty which enters the more intense movement of the episodes leading to the fall. The third stage will begin at the fall. Some of the materials in Adam's account we have discussed in the second chapter—chiefly the clear discovery of joy and gratitude and the unclear discovery of passion. We shall want to keep in view some aspects of the issues already taken up, for they are part of the cumulative background Milton constructs for his unprecedented story.

Before turning to the materials which lead to the formal

point of climax in the fall, however, we may take advantage of our present perspective to consider some things which will assist our understanding of where we have been and are still to go. Since the foreground of postlapsarian experience and interpretation is for the most part blocked off and denied direct and open application to events before the fall, Milton endows with special interest, and with potential, suggestive movement, the background he creates. Books VII and VIII are the first from which the Antagonist, hitherto prominent in the poem, is absent. Satan's precipitate departure "murmuring" in the last line of Book IV occurs in the narrative present. He returns to play a major role in the narrative past of Books V and VI, and the dream which he left behind him occupies the present of the first two hundred lines of Book V. Satan brings with him an extensive background exhibiting the consequences of wrong choice while further developing those consequences in his soliloquies. He furnishes the one background developed by narrative action which Milton can use to draw on postlapsarian experience while still staying within the strict rules of his story. (This is not to discount God's pronouncement in Book III, but foreknowledge would seem to have a somewhat different relation to events after the fall, and more "influence" perhaps, while saving and supporting the freedom which has faltered.)

The dream Satan produces within Eve is the most ominous forward step of the plot; it is also the only open and direct action that may be construed as an advance toward the expected climax. Everything else we have so far noticed is momentary or ambiguous, suggesting the possible in passing but with discontinuities and reserves which create tensions in the beholder and stimulate suspense, yet with no action either open or complete enough to be interpreted as a movement from the possible toward the probable. Eve's dream is interrupted by the angelic guard, countered by the human purgation of the morning prayer, and countered by the mission of Raphael. If other actions seem neither open nor complete, Eve's dream is complete enough to make it difficult to imagine how Satan could have improved his work if not interrupted. One may reasonably conclude that the author's absolute control of narrative time has cooperated with the villain to make the pre-temptation as effective as possible; for the interruption is, however natural in appearance, a calculated one on the part of the author, who made this choice on his own. As a result the broken dream has its own subtle form of completeness, a stimulating suggestion implanted and invited to grow on its own, as everyone's natural wit can recognize. Both the dream and the form of its presentation are of course useful to the story in its commitment to trial and the exercise of freedom.

In contrast to the lack of openness in other actions, Eve's dream is left so entirely open that in weight and proportion its ambiguity exceeds whatever else we have observed— including Adam's discovery of passion and the subsequent exchanges which, in spite of and partly because of the rigidity and conclusiveness of debate, remain inconclusive in effect; and Raphael's brief, intense revelation of angelic sexuality, which is, like Eve's dream, broken off by the author's calculated control of narrative time. As episode Eve's dream is wholly clear in its aims, for between Ithuriel's discovery of the agent, "How busied, in what form and posture couched," and the explosive return of Satan to his "own likeness" the narrative voice intrudes nine lines of professional analysis which are so compact, precise, and authoritative that one may not be aware of the break the parenthesis makes in the action. Some two hundred lines later, characteristically filled by Milton with action that holds our immediate interest while relegating suspense to some undercurrent of our minds, Eve tells her dream to Adam. Though clear to us, the purposes of the dream are not so definitively translatable by Adam as Raphael's narration of the war in heaven and of the creation. Besides, Raphael's account is a full one, and he includes both internal and external commentary. In the case of the dream, however, Adam's understanding is temporarily limited by his innocence and by his lack of essential information, the existence and history of Satan, which he will soon receive to make possible the application of retrospective wisdom. How he will handle the trial of such knowledge is another problem, not on the schedule of the present exposition.

To sum up the problems at hand: Adam and Eve experience with anxiety and incomplete understanding the effects of the dream; Satan's purposes are fully understood and countered by divine action, though the response of heaven is limited by the established rules of freedom; both the aims of the dream and the nature of divine response are presumably open to the reader, who has been the witness of Satan's external career and internal conversations, and has been prompted by the poet's clear analysis of the aims of such dreamwork. When the reader finally hears Eve's account of her nocturnal experience, he recognizes the acting out of a familiar language of symbolic states and suggestions. From his perspective of narrative knowledge and human experience, he can translate the indirectness of the dream language with assurance. But the reader's understanding will prove to be a kind of misplaced fortress, dominant in its outlook but unable by benefit of elevation either to influence or to observe clearly the significance of the action which takes place a little out of reach. For the language acted out in the dream is not opposed (except once, briefly) and is not developed in the same terms as the original presentation. We must wait through another third of the poem before we have the opportunity to make a direct connection with the import of the dream, but then the terms will not be the same. We can sift the offered materials furnished by Adam's disclosure of his waking dream of passion, and by the debate concerning the advisability of dividing work in the Garden, and by Satan's temptation of Eve—and use these to compose a fabric of reference and hypotheses, but we cannot make these coincide with the language of the dream in ways that will provide clear and certain satisfaction.

Let us look at some of the action following the dream before we return to put our problems into a context which may be answerable to Milton's narrative intentions. In part of the effort by Adam and Eve to counter their experience we may observe the narrator making a choice which involves difficulties but which, we may suppose, he did not expect the reader to misunderstand. The morning prayer offered by Adam and Eve is correct in form, though without benefit of the Psalms or later models, and intended also as poetic propaganda against set prayers. The "unmeditated" prayer does what the best religious wisdom prescribes in such circumstances—renews and affirms essential faith in God by heartfelt praise. That wisdom would not regard their limited understanding of the dream, its import and secret intention, as a major handicap. Since the real issue is alienation from God, fundamental to all disobedience, first and subsequent, their turning toward God in an exercise of concentrated attention to the manifest signs of God's presence in the world would act as pledge, would renew any unconscious wavering in their dedication, and by removing the fertile ground of felt anxiety would ward off the kind of mortal blow which could fall only on the unguarded heart.

When Adam and Eve conclude—

> *and if the night*
> *Have gathered aught of evil or concealed,*
> *Disperse it, as now light dispels the dark.*
> *(V, 206–08)*

—we have no position within the rules and values of the poem from which we could criticize the prayer and regard it as, for instance, perhaps too trusting or even complacent. A position outside the poem would need to undertake something more than a critical interpretation or a revision like Bentley's; an ambitious enterprise might find itself gradually rewriting the whole poem in prose, to modernize the values and liberate the implications hidden from a less enlightened and more fearful age, as if the story were some rich but carelessly mined myth waiting for the right story-teller to rescue its buried possibilities. This can be done and has been done, to greater and lesser degree, and is almost always interesting to criticism, and often provocatively valuable, but the extensively rewritten story of *Paradise Lost* is likely to have the embarrassing handicap of being as story a piece of inferior art.

When the narrative voice declares:

> *So prayed they innocent, and to their thoughts*
> *Firm peace recovered soon and wonted calm.*
> *(V, 209–10)*

we seem obliged to accept the poet's word, which, as not always, he takes the pains to corroborate with the testimony of significant action, human and divine. Adam and Eve turn to their gardening, and the tasks named would appear to reflect their present state in response to their recent experience. They prune those fruit trees which are "over-woody" and need "hands to check / Fruitless embraces" of "pampered boughs." Here we surely have in another sphere of activity a symbolic, tentative answer to the efforts of Satan's dream to produce illusions and raise

> *discontented thoughts,*
> *Vain hopes, vain aims, inordinate desires*
> *Blown up with high conceits engend'ring pride.*
> *(IV, 807–09)*

The language of symbolic action, at least now, does directly oppose the meanings and intentions concealed in the action of the dream. The activity opposing fruitless growth is also a suggestive reminder of the larger problem of the moral drama, in which the full liberty of innocence nevertheless depends upon honoring one symbolic, absolute restriction. The second activity named is a form of creative working with God; in the language of the prayer:

> *In these thy lowest works, yet these declare*
> *Thy goodness beyond thought, and power divine.*
> *(V, 158–59)*

They wed the fruit-bearing vine to the elm as a re-enactment of their own marriage and of their participation "In honor to the world's great Author." Male and female, negative and positive seem to be summed up in these two simple acts which follow the narrative voice's announcement of restored peace and calm.

At this point God, apparently not satisfied by the assurance of the relatively omniscient narrator, beholds the couple with pity and sends Raphael on his errand of conversational friendship. We are not told whether God's pity is prompted by some residual human distress which the narrator cannot see or does not wish to take the responsibility for seeing, or whether God's response answers the Providential view of the fruit which Satan's night gardening will bring forth. The pity is seminal but remains within the mind of God without further expression. No doubt we are intended to infer that man's initiative in prayer and work not only precedes grace but is answered by it—even with no spelling out of the details and conditions which govern the relationship. Only after the fall can prevenient grace make a formal entrance into the world. Pity is mentioned by the narrator but not explained; most of God's speech to Raphael concerns the practical instructions to Adam: the thrice-repeated subject of free will, the danger of feeling "too secure," and the warning that Satan's attack will take the form of "deceit and lies." In conclusion, justice is adumbrated by God and named by the narrator, more emphatically than pity, and with a Providential turn which to our coarser human hearing may sound more minatory than regretful.

Yet if we step back from the intricacies of discrimination, the main lines of narrative intention are clear. God's pity is definite evidence of the effectiveness of the human prayer and work, corroborating the narrator's bare statement that peace and calm returned "soon" after the prayer. Peace and calm are not superficial attributes, least of all in the present circumstances, and the poet cannot consciously intend any reservations or half-truths on such issues. Nor can he wish to make God and His pity subject to the subtle refluxes of a character acting in a personal drama.[6] Serious doubts at this juncture are likely to be radical ones that challenge Milton's understanding of the human issues involved and challenge his concept of the divine. The poet's own involvement in the imaginative action is of course always a subject to be opened, though he may raise marvelous obstructions to our view. But if we cannot believe the plain accuracy of his statement on peace and calm, his hold on the story and on the reader will have slipped dangerously.

The episode of the dream and its aftermath deserves all the attention we can bring to bear.[7] In the suggestive latencies, in the meeting of the human actors, the demonic, the divine, and the mediating poet, we may observe a crucial action and a characteristic solution by the poet-narrator. The only overt action that might serve as a firm bridge to the Eve of Book IX is the dream which Milton took the care to produce with great skill and then to leave entirely open. We can hardly think that he expected his readers to ignore or forget that episode, or to fail to observe his pointed silence. Milton's narrative procedure, on a large scale here, is the basic method we have had many occasions to observe: the creating of suspense through delay, interruption, discontinuity, and suggestion countered by reservation. The main technique seems to be deliberate, a chosen way to tell the story, both for the sake of the story—no small matter—and for the truths of which it is the vehicle.

The effects of Eve's dream help confirm the practice we have seen elsewhere. After the dream Adam and Eve are, as before, exposed to trial; they stand once again "On even ground." According to the rules of the story, what has always been possible has received a rehearsal in dream and has been rejected awake. The possible is therefore no more probable in the daylight theater of action. If the veteran reader of tales, who happens to know the outcome of this story, has an unauthorized sense of movement toward the probable, he is left on his own to "overmaster" it as he may; or at least to struggle with the educated sense that the conflict is within him and his own acquired habits of understanding, and not within the characters he is privileged to oversee. His normal fictional privilege only increases personal tension and suspense if he intelligently resists attributing his own dark knowledge prematurely. This experience, as we have seen and shall see further, is a standard though varied effect of Milton's narrative art.

What is chiefly different is a matter of proportion. After the sudden irruption of Satan's making the first positive move toward his end, the flow of human action is put into a kind of reservoir. A change of tempo and a vast imbalance slow the developing story almost to a standstill, as the counter-activity of heaven produces the background of a grand digression which is likely to cause restless impatience in the simple lover of continuous narrative. The fit reader will perhaps recognize that once again his literary patience is being taught and tempered to an unusual degree, as Raphael's afternoon extends across more than a fourth of the poem. As for the calculated imbalance of the dream, presented in Book IV and impending until Book IX, it is but one of many imbalances Milton cultivates. Within the episode of Raphael's visit there is the relative leisure of Adam's personal story, and then the sudden disclosure of passion and the enigmatic revelation of angelic sexuality which quickly return the end of the episode to a narrative mood and tempo resembling the place where the line of action broke off, the episode of the dream. To glance ahead: Eve's temptation and fall are fully staged; Adam capitulates in a dozen lines. But the largest imbalance is the one that begins in Book III, with the revelation of the Son's new kind of love, as sacrifice, which cannot be mentioned by Raphael and can begin to show its effects only when there is a beloved sinner to be saved.

Whatever Milton's own narrative pleasure in delay and complex equilibrium, the nature of the story to be told and his obligation to the truths he would justify are well answered by the procedures he has chosen. The principle "that great / Or bright infers not excellence" is a principle freely applicable to both narrative proportions and the moral universe of the poem. At the doctrinal level, for instance, Milton must constantly emphasize limits. At the narrative level, Satan is free to steal much of the show, and he can work inside to tempt the will. The obligation of God's justice extends only to making certain that Adam's mind is "sufficient," and possesses the basic information to work upon. Once Adam has demonstrated the capability of his mind and will, the will is out of bounds, as it were, the sacred center of freedom which neither God nor an emissary of God will try to influence directly apart from understanding. So Raphael is, fortunately, not asked for advice on the content of Eve's dream. Instead he tells the history of Satan and the story of creation, from which Adam and Eve are intelligent enough to draw all necessary conclusions. These are few and brief, and could be summarized in less space even than Adam's concluding speech in Book XII, and could be carved with room to spare on a medium-sized apple.

Book IX opens with the poet's last invocation to the Muse and last extended personal statement, followed by the necessary return of Satan, who has been gone for seven days. Since Raphael departed at the close of Book VIII, six days of narrative silence have elapsed. The fatal morning begins with a brief thematic reminiscence of the great hymn of praise answering the trouble of a week ago:

> *Now whenas sacred light began to dawn*
> *In Eden on the humid flow'rs, that breathed*
> *Their morning incense, when all things that breathe*
> *From th' earth's great altar send up silent praise*
> *To the Creator, and his nostrils fill*
> *With grateful smell, forth came the human pair*
> *And joined their vocal worship to the quire*
> *Of creatures wanting voice.*
> *(IX, 192–99)*

Then without warning Eve broaches her suggestion that they divide their morning's work.

To judge by the quantity and quality of critical argument on record, the episode is one of the most successful Milton wrote. What follows will not at long last present the correct and comprehensive interpretation of what does happen or should have happened, but will benefit from the example of prior endeavors chiefly by undertaking a briefer way through the entanglements. To some extent the diversity of critical opinion is made possible, perhaps inevitable, by the cumulative narrative reticences which Milton has been holding in balance.[8] For example, if we wish to name as motivating cause for Eve's abrupt dissatisfaction anything given formal shape by the plot, we must look to the delayed effects of the dream inspired by Satan. Milton, who is not always reluctant to give didactic directions, is completely silent on the issue, and the reader will receive no confirmation that his guess is accurate or sufficient. If we wish to name a single reason for Adam's eventual giving in to Eve, we are put in a similar position. We have nothing more substantial to nominate than Adam's disclosure of passion. Both causes, though adequate in the abstract, when considered as separate episodes presented their own initial difficulties of interpretation, as we have observed at length. To compound matters, if these are indeed the motivating causes, they are masked by the dialogue between Adam and Eve, for Milton avoids any direct echoes that we can link with the dream or the disclosure of passion. The discovery of indirect echoes will depend upon the uncertainties of psychological interpretations, perhaps over-encouraged by a wealth of new material in an unprecedented situation without background and with indistinct controls. We may even wonder, in a moment of useless distraction, what happened during the six days the narrative suddenly passed over. The reader's general position of uncertainty is one Milton has arranged many times, but now far more is at stake.

For this scene Milton employs a technique partly adumbrated before but different in degree and in effect. The chief precedent is the episode of exchanges between Adam and Raphael on the subject of passion, characterized by some tone of debate and by some exaggerations and omissions that suggested less than a full meeting of minds. The scene of Raphael's arrival provides a lesser precedent, with its hints of domestic friction and its display of Adam forgetting to be tactful. The ultimate model for dialogue is heard only in heaven, but is translated into the practicable terms of a Socratic prototype in the exchanges between Adam and his Creator which lead to the idea of Eve. Yet this dialogue, though it sets a measurable standard for Adam's other performances, remains a solitary ideal never again attained.

In Book IX Adam finds himself in an unexpected dialogue initiated by Eve. All his previous experience with her has been based upon intellectual privilege and deference. He has led discussions and offered impromptu lectures, and we have been informed by a deliberate narrative aside that she has enjoyed Adam's instructional methods:

> *he, she knew, would intermix*
> *Grateful digressions, and solve high dispute*
> *With conjugal caresses; from his lip*
> *Not words alone pleased her.*
> *(VIII, 54–57)*

What begins with the air of dialogue quickly turns into something else. The initiative is never quite regained by Adam, though he tries, and the discussion moves without clear leadership or control as Eve's practical suggestion turns into a major test of their relations and of much more. Undercurrents, the sources of which are not visible but invite speculation, move their statements about in unanticipated ways that seem nevertheless convincing in their effects. Adam on the defensive cannot keep their differences from drifting and broadening as Eve's modest proposal becomes a crisis that calls everything into question.

So much by way of introduction to the problems of the scene. As for the short cut I propose to take: this will consist of concentrating chiefly on two statements by Adam which will provide, I believe, some larger illumination of the context while reflecting additional light on issues we have been following. When Eve suggests that they busy themselves in different parts of the Garden in order to avoid the work-wasting interruptions of smiles, looks, and casual talk, Adam defends the rights and dues of their life together. With no discernible reservations on Milton's part, Adam explains that talk refreshes and nourishes the mind, that smiles are the exchange of reason, "and are of love the food, / Love not the lowest end of human life." The defense is quiet, soothing, and correct, a preface to the main point:

> *For not to irksome toil, but to delight*
> *He made us, and delight to reason joined.*
> *(IX, 242–43)*

This is the first statement to be considered, and it is a detached summary of Adam's true experience in responding to the first sense of joy, and is therefore a renewed confirmation of the simple truth and of his conscious control of that truth. In spite of the ambiguities and dangers revealed in his effort to express the inward sense of passion first discovered, Adam here seems to justify the confidence that his feelings "subject not . . . Who meet with various objects . . . Variously representing; yet still free, / Approve the best, and follow what I approve." If delight and reason are *not* joined, Adam would seem to be averring to Raphael, he will of course follow reason. To this point Paradise has offered no occasion for such a choice. Even the dialogue in which Adam found himself taking a position apparently opposed to that of his Creator finally discovered that the "heart's desire" and reason were at one. It is true that God with gentle wit emphasized the stubbornness of Adam's insistence on delight:

> *A nice and subtle happiness, I see,*
> *Thou to thyself proposest, in the choice*
> *Of thy associates, Adam, and wilt taste*
> *No pleasure, though in pleasure, solitary.*
> *(VIII, 399–402)*

Whatever Providential irony is in the remark, the immediate purpose, which satisfies God's intention and Milton's narrative art, is to make a transition. Adam has spoken well of the nature of fellowship, which is "mutual" and participates in "rational delight." The next subject God puts forward to test Adam's intelligence and will is solitude, and Adam proves himself a ready theologian, but he shows no inclination to discuss the merits of solitude for man. The circumstances do not require his developing that side of the subject, and there is no "felt" omission, as there well may be in Adam's neither defending nor simply rejecting his praise of passion. Yet the example illustrates once more Milton's capacity to make the unsaid register its presence in a story which, like any good story but to a far greater degree, cannot tell all.

In his new kind of conversation with his "other self" Adam finds that he is opposing a position based upon a declared separation between reason and delight. Eve, with a fascinating stubbornness which resembles, with differences, that of her "other self" arguing with God, rejects delight and insists on reason, or her version of reason. In this trial the limits are lifted. There is no gracious voice of God to say, "Thus far to try thee, Adam, I was pleased." Nor does the scene register as a wholly fictional trial. It seems to move closer to real consequences than the imaginative effort by Adam to explain how Eve's loveliness makes him feel about wisdom, higher knowledge, reason, and authority. Among the many difficulties Adam encounters, not the least is that of trying to defend delight to an "other self" who for the moment is all at once unresponsive to his interests and remains politely unpersuaded. An agreement taken for granted suddenly vanishes, and if the value of delight is not shared its worth has been denied. Eve never responds to his restatement of principle— "delight to reason joined"—and by her effective silence on the point, and by her evident interest in other points, a discussion turns into a disagreement. It does not turn into a quarrel, and it is useless to borrow from later wisdom to improve the story and prevent disaster. Both participants exercise restraint, in different ways which both help and hinder a possible clarification of the issue between them, while preventing the open rupture which might lead to an easier solution.

Milton is introducing, as for the first time, a problem now grown familiar. There is no easy agreement on fundamental things and soon none upon limits. The issues escalate in silent transitions as Eve raises the question of happiness and Adam answers with a defense of freedom. He may speak the truth well enough, but he does not see the ways in which his language describes himself and his present choices, for he is only now beginning to experience the possible complications of applying the principles of freedom to himself when not in agreement with his "other self." In the face of Eve's resolution Adam retreats from his unified sense of the order of reason and feeling, to save appearances with an apparently rational compromise, the paradoxical "Go; for thy stay, not free, absents thee more." He seems to have won the rational part of the argument (though we can see the submerged other part in Eve's apparent refusal to be persuaded) when he suddenly reverses himself to surrender, without acknowledging it, to Eve's will. Though innocent, Adam moves toward the threshold of the fallen world and exhibits what looks like an inclination toward tragic consequences—an inclination only, for he is still free to draw back though we may doubt that he will. The recognition that he has made a symbolic half-step forward and must draw back does not derive from the foreground of fallen experience, at least not entirely; we may claim some authorization from the background which Milton has carefully constructed. To look ahead: the way Adam has solved the first serious conflict by translating the issue—with a questionable sense of proportion—into a domestic model of freedom does not augur well for the decisive test which awaits. To look back: we remember Adam under the self-induced pressure of trying to find words for the inward sense of passion, and how he then translated the language of feeling into the language of knowledge, and though in a fiction transposed the values of knowledge.

We can see these issues and their subtle motions but Adam cannot, and for two equally valid reasons. He *is* innocent and lacks our expensive knowledge of human nature. He *is* involved in the scene he is acting, more completely and less consciously than his acting out the disclosure of passion; he is involved more deeply than he realizes and in ways he does not understand, in ways that perhaps we do not understand though we are well supplied with explanations. The perspective and detachment which permit us to see, though with conscious restraints, the possibilities of tragic consequences, allow us to recognize, with less intervening restraint, something a little older and much renewed in human history, the *beginnings* of tragic experience itself.

In responding to Eve's initiative Adam reveals more of what moves him, for Milton has seen to it that we know far more about Adam—for reasons which combine traditional thought, doctrine, and the selective purposes of a dramatic presentation. Though Eve takes the lead, her motives are less available for scrutiny. She may therefore be more open to free-ranging speculative analysis. If, however, we do not compose a psychological sub-plot out of insights and experience claiming a timeless wisdom (and otherwise not really different in critical authority and historical license from the foreground of traditional thought and experience which Milton has endeavored to keep inoperative, a source of tension at one remove from the story and behind a sort of glass wall); if we do not piece together a sub-plot for Eve, then we have nothing more substantial to invoke as her motive than the dream inspired by Satan. The critical problem stimulates but resists various intellectual desires for satisfaction, but is by no means unusual in dramatic literature where we often find an immense disparity between a nominal motive and a closely integrated sequence of action powerfully convincing in its development and effect. The scene of slight domestic friction upon the arrival of the angelic guest, and Adam's gesture in dividing their work for that occasion may be considered as a suggestive precedent perhaps, but not a motive. The same would be true of the observation that Eve's desire to work separate is a reversion to *her* first experience of delight, her pleasure in the "answering looks / Of sympathy and love" produced by her reflection in the "clear / Smooth lake, that to me seemed another sky." Adam's looks are of course not "answering" right, as they did before, and there is no divine voice to intervene and correct her error.

We come now to our second statement. It follows the defense of delight and reason, with only a brief and neutral change of subject in between. Adam says:

> But if much converse perhaps
> Thee satiate, to short absence I could yield.
> For solitude sometimes is best society,
> And short retirement urges sweet return.
> (IX, 247–50)

The currents of feeling suggested would seem to resemble those produced in Adam's account of how the discovery of passion affected him. Now he is not "acting," not making a sustained imaginative effort to disclose "What inward thence I feel, not therefore foiled." Though he withdraws the suggestion at once, thinking of the enemy outside, that act of judgment, while certainly not a diversion, is nevertheless clearly not directed toward the feelings themselves. (The example is one more illustration of Milton's cultivated art of the unsaid.) Adam cannot imagine an enemy inside.

The suggestion is advanced and withdrawn, but the significance is not withdrawn. First there is the unmistakable failure of nerve, the lover's private suggestion of fear that the food of love, the looks, smiles, talk, may have satiated the beloved one. The ironies are multiple, reverberating against his opening statement which describes the nourishment of reason in love and declares the unity of delight and reason; there are besides those principles of temperance in food and knowledge, which if applied here are done so most oddly and askew; then there are the recollections of passion, which makes loveliness appear "so absolute . . . And in herself complete." Our first view of Adam described him as formed for contemplation and valor. We are witnessing in the failure of nerve the limits of valor. Contemplation, the fruits of which Adam has never appeared slow in offering to Eve, makes the next move: "For solitude sometimes is best society." This, the first historical appearance of a famous quotation, never less alone than when alone, is in the context a dubious aphorism. It may presage "Go; for thy stay, not free, absents thee more," that translation of the general laws of freedom into a convenient domestic model.

By anticipating the famous quotation Milton seems willing, at this point, to admit foreground associations of solitude with contemplation. Perhaps he is even glancing at those progressive seventeenth-century "gardenists" who praised and promoted the value of scientific work and thought in gardens, as an intellectual *aggiornamento* of the old value of contemplative withdrawal.[9] (And Marvell, at least, would have enjoyed recognizing that inclination of Adam to imagine a Paradise within Paradise, where the unity of delight and reason might be safe.) But these effects are at most the sport of the author, briefly touching barely audible echoes out of time. The protagonist himself seems to be engrossed in trying out a mildly intellectualized suggestion, in order to answer, or substitute for, "What inward thence" Eve may be feeling—if she is indeed overburdened with the nourishment of his talk and company. As in the use of a domestic model of freedom, Adam is "weighing" her with himself, though not quite as Raphael advised.[10] At least, the "self-esteem" is dubiously "grounded on just and right / Well managed." Instead, "realities" would seem to be seeking graceful ways of yielding to "shows." For Adam has no trouble deciding against separation. What baffles him is how to convince Eve, or, failing that, how to mollify her feelings, or, failing that, how to convince his reason that it is not following the will, whether his or hers. When he dallies with a thought of the sweet uses of solitude, he is inventing a reason that may satisfy reason.

The sudden discovery of the human value of solitude is a novelty that fits, much too well, the pressures of the occasion. Adam seems to forget what the rules of this story will not condone, a clear demonstration of knowledge from which there can be no honorable retreat—his passionate reasoning to God on the difference between divine solitude and the human need for fellowship. But the corollary to the justification for solitude is Adam's most startling invention: "And short retirement urges sweet return." Reason seems here, though unawares, fully in the service of pleasure, as the argument for solitude becomes a convenient gesture between the husband's fear that he is boring his wife and the "short absence," "short retirement," that will make the heart grow fonder. In his anxiety Adam has discovered a fortunate fall peculiarly suitable to lovers, one that turns "sweet reluctant amorous delay" into the stimulating contrivance of "short retirement" for purposes of "sweet return."

What should Adam have done? The question tends to honor the story by forgetting that it is a story, and by making it as "real" and immediate as something we might have to decide for ourselves in an academic debate of conscience. The question has received some serious, perhaps over-serious, consideration in recent years.[11] A few instances may have been stimulated by dissatisfaction with the argument of *Answerable Style*, which was not so much wrong as excessively right, the characteristic pursuit by an author of middle years of the one path he was tracing through dusky woods. The question, if not chased beyond the stretch of the story, is a legitimate one, for the temper of narrative inevitability is always improved by some peripheral vision, at least, of saving alternatives.

Adam might have tried insisting on Eve's obedience. He does raise, and stress, the issue—just before he retreats from his own reason. (He wavers only on the tentative subject of solitude, and he makes the impromptu bridge by accepting Eve's suggestion, rather hastily "interpreted" by Adam to give it a slight prudential cast—that one may be better prepared and less over-confident when the trial is deliberately sought.) Neither the governing rules of the story nor the rights of a seventeenth-century husband impose any real obstructions to Adam's forcing the issue of obedience. She could have disobeyed freely and of course would have had to, or the poet would have had to try again with a better plan. The literal base of the historical story cannot be violated, though anxious Adam does not know this, and is worried that "the sweet of life" seems to be interrupted by something "remote," "obscure and subtle," which nevertheless both concerns and lies before him "in daily life." But had the issue been drawn it would have meant, at the least, less involvement by Adam in her exposure and fall. If this had happened, it might have constituted a proto-legal separation and initial grounds for divorce, which the writer of those infamous divorce tracts could have shown as a solution that would have prevented "all our woe" and not merely domestic woe. Milton's capacity to imagine destruction is immense but discriminating, and he will not diminish by so much as the weight of a narrative thread any of the force implicit in the realization of the story. Even if we ignore the doctrinal fine points, while trying to give Eve all her due, we must recognize that she is not the tragic protagonist of the story Milton writes. Though a necessary tragic accomplice—like Shakespeare's Lady Macbeth—the full, essential failure is Adam's, whose experience precedes, involves, encompasses, and exceeds hers.[12]

A less damaging fictional alternative for Adam would have been to say less; that is, to stop short of his little speech on freedom and to wait out her sweet displeasure. With characteristic art Milton raises the possibility of Adam's insisting on *obedience* just before the hero backs away. And Milton lets the possibility of Adam's having withheld *permission* flash out just after Adam has bid her go, with a brief benediction and exhortation that echoes Raphael's last words to him. "So spake the patriarch of mankind"—and the archhusband—still, it would seem, hopefully expecting Eve to honor the spirit of his generous, reluctant approval. A moment of silent tension occurs, a tipping of human scales in no "celestial sign":

> but Eve
> *Persisted; yet submiss, though last, replied:*
> *With thy permission then.*
> *(IX, 376–78)*

She goes the "willinger" because "forewarned," chiefly by the delicate hint in his "last reasoning words," which she paraphrases from his opportune translation of her own words. Milton's narrative art works against the leisure of reflection at this point, but we have arrived at a moment of elevation from which we can look back and swiftly recognize the distance traveled from a similar elevation: the first auditory image of himself which Eve presented to Adam when she quoted the "pleaded reason" of his original love speech. In this latest image of Adam she has "infused" her own image and can quote the beauty of her wisdom as from a reflecting surface. "What thou hast said is just and right"—this tag might still be applied, but it did take Adam an unusually long time, even for him, to say the right thing.

It is clear that Adam's not withholding of permission is a personal fault, an error of will and judgment to be deplored and understood, but by that queer audience which is composed of admiring connoisseurs of stories, to be applauded. If Adam had withheld permission, and Milton had not planned all along to do the necessary job in still another scene, Eve would still have had to go. Adam's involvement in her fate would then have been greater than if he had demanded obedience and been denied, but less than it is by his granting reluctant permission. If she had gone, against his declared judgment but neither held back nor released by his will, the final decision of the climactic scene would have appeared, as we approached it, more open and evenly balanced than it now is. The moment of decision would generate the same degree of pressure, but without the sense of tightening that is now produced by the dramatic expectation that there is only one last chance to reverse the intimations of psychological movement. The kind of reversal of judgment and will Adam displays in the present scene might gain some benefit in surprise if postponed to the final decision, but would then lose the support of the cumulative—still "free" and off-the-record, as it were—presentiments which Milton has been showing in a suggestive pattern of "foreknowledge" which refrains from overt "influence." Milton might well have weighed these possibilities but would have known that a climax is too late for unprecedented new action, and that valid surprise must emerge from the grain. The inevitable may then throw off its last disguises, but these must satisfy as remembered evidence one did not need to accept or quite recognize, but are now in a time and place where they cannot be denied. New evidence may surprise and still convince, as a legal maneuver, but an answer to be felt as justice will want to convince more deeply than the maneuvers of surprise make possible.

Within the constrictions of his story and its rules Milton has managed to invent still another premonition of the fall that does not cross the boundary of innocence. For suggestions Milton may draw upon Eve's dream and Adam's disclosure of his passion—models partly in their substance and

partly in their thematic design, both of which lend themselves to variations that suggest their source, but at some
indefinite remove and without direct quotation. As if in a
dream, or a consciously acted illusion, the characters re-
hearse the fall in a fable, as it were, and exhibit a trial version
of what will happen as if it is certain. A narrowing margin in
reality is nevertheless preserved. The trial version is *not* the
fall, and the alternative conclusions (Adam's freedom to de-
mand obedience or withhold permission), expressed just before and after the actual conclusion, show that there is no
internal necessity that the episode should have ended exactly
as it does. Besides, this is not Milton's last invention; what
finally does happen, at the real crisis, will not duplicate this
version but will again introduce variation.

The temptation of Eve is a full-dress performance, operatic
in its lavish artifice, elegance, and fullness. Satan bestows on
Eve all the benefits of a great actor in his most famous role,
now being played for the first time. The scene is a deliberate
archetype of the history, traditions, imitations, and developments of the flourishing literature of temptation. Many
of Milton's intricate voices[13] heard in the raising of Pandemonium, and inside, outside, and elsewhere, and in his art
of composing high, sustained extravagance that weaves its
bright threads of mockery into darker patterns, are now heard
again—varied, transformed, and extended by inventions appropriate to a new stage toward which all preparations and
practice have been aiming.

From the author's point of view the excess has more than
one purpose to fulfill. Satan can act, not only as if he is writing
a story or interpreting a script, but is making history, and he
is. He is also acting in character, as master of the politics of
hell, where opposition is always overwhelmed by varieties of
excess—including the apparent patience of hearing out a long
debate, the soothing fullness of oratory, the briefer eloquence
of tears, the exact brevity of the answer that forestalls an
unspoken question, or crushes (as Satan does in answering
Beelzebub)[14] a question raised. As master of the instruments
of hypocrisy, he has acted out in speeches to himself the need
to lie to himself which is fundamental to his mastery.

Though Satan renews and intensifies a few resonances
from Eve's dream, as we should expect, and with a sinister
sureness of touch we expect, we are not allowed to think that
the success of the temptation depends in a crucial way upon

the groundwork of the dream. The timing which Milton has provided is of course very favorable to the seductive enterprise. But Satan's individual efforts are intended to go so far beyond the groundwork and the opportune timing that they may seem quite sufficient to overwhelm a somewhat restless woman of carefully limited experience and nurture, out alone for the first time, by virtue of her own efforts, toward which she may well feel some reckless flush of triumph, and perhaps misgiving. Satan's opportunity is made for him and is more advantageous than theories of justice would require. This must be acknowledged as an imperfection in theory if we wish to make Eve the separate and supreme test of justice, but it imposes no flaw on the story or on the matter of freedom. It must also be acknowledged that legalism has clear lines of defense. She is there by an act of her own will; she knows the basic facts; she has just won an argument with her husband, who has proved the excellence of his ability at the highest levels; nothing in the endowment of her original feminine nature prevents her from forming a negative word; she can leave with graceful haste and regard these matters of "high dispute" as not wholly unlike astronomy.

All of this notwithstanding, she is more of an instrument than a demonstration to "justify the ways of God to men." Milton has chosen to tell the story thus, and the choice is intrinsic in the whole design, whatever protests or suggested revisions may be proposed at this point. Her being so completely overmatched by Satan strains but does not violate the moral rules, and satisfies fictional plausibilities, and creates a tension between sympathy for her and fascinated shock as the perversities of human character begin to emerge. The episode is so interesting, and Satan has worked so well as author of his own rival story, that we may forget the suspense we ought to be feeling at this protracted preparation for the crucial scene that we know is coming.

Milton makes Eve's temptation unfold with such deliberate fullness that its time of telling, from Eve's leaving until she is "met" by Adam, comes within one hundred and fifty lines of being as long as each of the three shortest books of the poem. The writer who made this choice apparently believed in the expressive value of asymmetry and imbalance, and no doubt, being Milton, had moral thoughts on the subject. He also shows himself to be the kind of storyteller who enjoys the wit of commanding the reader's interest in the matter at hand, even though the decisive matter which the reader has been longing for, and which is now very close, cannot be brought forward until the present business, in its own good time, is consummated. Adam falls in a dozen lines. Yet this is the crux upon which everything depends. Nor is the poet free and exempt but is himself on trial—not his Muse, or "upright heart," or humility, but the man from whose mouth all the words have been written down, who has been binding himself, as poets can, with even more obligations than he avows. The climax must prove the rightness of his power to create and carry through a design that will bear the accumulating weight, that will answer the questions raised, left open, postponed, or embellished in a mist of ambiguity, the "common gloss" of poets and their critics. At this place he must make good some of the most important claims of his argument.

In a state of exhilaration Eve tells her story, the self-deceptions of which are chilling to the sober. But Adam, and the narrator, pointedly ignore such trifles. Adam's dismay[15] is directed at what the narrator names for him: "The fatal trespass done by Eve." Then the central, deciding speech takes place in Adam's mind:

> *O fairest of creation, last and best*
> *Of all God's works, creature in whom excelled*
> *Whatever can to sight or thought be formed,*
> *Holy, divine, good, amiable, or sweet!*
> *How art thou lost, how on a sudden lost,*
> *Defaced, deflow'red, and now to death devote!*
> *Rather how hast thou yielded to transgress*
> *The strict forbiddance, how to violate*
> *The sacred fruit forbidd'n! Some cursed fraud*
> *Of enemy hath beguiled thee, yet unknown,*
> *And me with thee hath ruined, for with thee*
> *Certain my resolution is to die.*
> *(IX, 896–907)*

The speech continues for a few lines, adding reasons why he cannot live without her. The reasons are those of his first passionate speech to Eve, persuading her not to return to her image in the pool but to the flesh and bone that gave her life. We heard that argument admiringly quoted by Eve in their first conversation of Book IV. Now the argument appears again in his inward speech, *after* the dramatic decision has been made. We are left at least partly on our own to judge the import of rational content and the evidence of timing as the narrative comment chooses to speak only of the effect: Adam feels "as one ... Recomforted ... Submitting to what seemed remediless."

The pathos of the echo, much favored in romantic opera, speaks eloquently for human love. There are other echoes, beautifully kept inconclusive until the "me with thee hath ruined." The opening lines in praise of Eve may appear to ratify the enthusiastic exaggerations that greeted the first sight of her after creation. But the only turn of mind not entirely sanctioned in that episode of first sight, after long searching, was the quickly withdrawn and qualified comparison of Eve with the meaner beauties of the Garden, which are about to be spurned again as "these wild woods forlorn." The echo of the speech explaining passion to Raphael may be thought closer to these opening lines, but still the praise of a lover, if the mood is elegiac and lamenting loss, cannot be taken in a strictly literal way. The exaggerations are dangerous, and one may suspect a hint of direction in "Holy, divine, good, amiable, or sweet," but still one cannot be certain what that formal order of correctly descending value means as it comes closer to the personal. ("Amiable" does not have its bland modern meaning, and "sweet" is part of Adam's personal vocabulary of love: the first sight of Eve "infused / Sweetness into my heart, unfelt before.") The past tense of "excelled" suggests the elegiac; the present tense of "can" seems to deny that he is looking backward in praise of what was. Then the direct admission of loss, intensified by its unexpected suddenness, would seem to stabilize what is felt as doubtful or wavering in direction. A strong and direct expression of lament moves the personal tenderness toward a recognition of the hard facts of conclusiveness and irreversibility, and then toward the language of judgment:

> Rather how hast thou yielded to transgress
> The strict forbiddance, how to violate
> The sacred fruit forbidd'n!

At this point Adam seems exactly where he was in the debate with Eve when he declared, "approve / First thy obedience." What should come now, if he is to repeat the previous pattern, is a display of reason that may serve to "satisfy" reason. Instead, Milton gives us an Adam who has passed beyond such deceptions. He knows at once without taking

her patter seriously that she must have been deceived and
that he does not know by whom or how. His expression of
understanding comes as a simple act, a kind of intellectual
reflex at once proving the possession and fulfilling the normal
nature of intelligence.[16] The "yet unknown" suggests the
intention of finding out, and a future, but trails away as an
uncompleted last act of knowledge, not so much broken
off—like so many of Milton's calculated interruptions of the
story—as abandoned. There is no sudden reversal of direction
now; there has been a brief dramatic poising of the issue, and
we are made to feel this in the language he uses to himself,
but we cannot tell whether the suspended moment is "real"
or "allegoric": he *is* deciding, but not by any formal process of
reasoning. Then he turns to embrace ruin without pretending
that he has the approval of his reason or that he is acting in the
name of freedom.

One result, which is a credit to Milton's artistic and human
generosity, is that when the moment which opens into general destruction comes, Adam is allowed to salvage something not unimportant, the human dignity of not lying to
himself as he goes down. His deception is full and comprehensive now, but it significantly lacks—and we have the
right to observe this—a particular dimension firmly established by the Satanic example and background, the use of
reason to deceive itself.

In Satan there is the metaphysical irony of his need to spin
out reason in ways that confirm the origin he would deny.
What begins as cosmic rebellion demonstrates the simple
force of truth, and to go on, to act, he must lie to himself. He
cannot escape the universal law which the habits of his mind,
however obliquely or faintly, still reflect. But Adam's act has
a special character unique in the poem: *simple* in the
philosophical sense that the one act comprehends a vast order
of consequences and is at the same time the symbol that
contains the whole retrospective betrayal of God and self.
According to the established psychological paradigm, Adam
rebels against his moral nature and his intellectual nature,
against will and understanding. Knowledge is abandoned,
simply displaced, "forgotten," and with it Adam's magnanimous correspondence with God in gratitude, love, and
devotion of "heart and voice and eyes." Knowledge is abandoned and love is betrayed for love. Adam enjoys the unprecedented liberty of a great personal leap beyond the "sanctity

of reason." Whatever reason can say in truthfully judging his love for Eve, the force of that love is such that it can deny, if only for a moment, the established laws of God's universe and does not need the mind to produce a deceiving knowledge. Adam's act is not, as that of Satan proves to be, a common rebellion that obeys truth while attempting to subvert it. At the decisive moment Adam is free of the compulsion that requires the apologetic mind of Satan to lie and reason and to invent steps and translations. Adam's act is unique, as it should be if it is to mean all that it has been thought to mean, and if it is to deserve an unprecedented act of providential mercy. Great sinners, even "holy" ones, will but imitate him subsequently, at a distance.[17]

We cannot, without rebelling against the truths of the story, think that Adam is in any sustainable way better than he was when innocent, but we perhaps do not need to suppress all sense of relief. The reader who has had to see, but strain not to acknowledge, the trials conducted under special circumstances may deserve some relief. If God's justice and providence have been presented as working in accord with the ways of dramatic truth, by gradual evolvement, one may expect that divine dramatic reason will not differ in kind (or abrogate the principle of accommodation) but will resemble human reason, and one may therefore expect some compensation to accompany Adam's tragic experience. Though man is to be saved entirely by grace, there ought to be something of worth to save. What God's providence finally achieves may be called a second creation, but only by way of pious metaphor; in effect it is a radical reformation and does not begin from the beginning again.

I pause to look back in a summary view and to observe some implications that are more visible in retrospect. The chief restrictions and obligations of Milton's narrative are those announced by God in Book III. "Foreknowledge" will not "influence" the future human violation of the "Sole pledge" of obedience. Though they are "deceived" by Satan and are not like him "self-depraved" by self-originating "suggestion," Adam and Eve are declared to be capable of resisting Satan, and must therefore be "authors to themselves in all / Both what they judge and what they choose." The laws of freedom are also part of the divine criterion of love, which requires active judging and choosing, not the "passive" service of necessity. Add to these obligations Milton's own announced purpose of asserting Providence and justifying God's ways to men. The demonstration of justice is directly and thoroughly involved in the actions leading to the fall; the assertion of Providence cannot in the same ways, however, be tied to details which men may examine and measure by the standards of justice they have learned from God and men. (I have some assertions of my own on the subject, as part of the argument of the last chapter.)

Milton borrows from his concept of the angelic fall, that original evil of self-suggestion, and surrounds Adam and Eve with suggestions. Most of these are of their own making (the poet variously assisting), and are not themselves evil but are the matter of trial, which is presented as normal, part of the nature of this universe. The suggestions are authorized and governed by the rules of "foreknowledge" and "influence," and by the laws of freedom inherent in fiction as Milton practices the art, and by other rules under the general name of decorum.

Among the "suggestions" we have discussed, though not from the present point of view, are the following: visual and auditory images of self-love; the dream from without implanted by Satan; the waking dreams of Adam, suggesting a first uneducated impulse to reject the good for the better and not to assimilate all into his magnanimous correspondence with heaven; the suggestions entertained in acting out the happy feelings of passion in a dramatic invention that rejects wisdom for beauty and enjoys the sensations thereby produced, or pretends to do some of this in a kind of waking dream of experimental fiction; the revelation of unimagined union in the higher love of angels; the suggestion of solitude in the debate with Eve, withdrawn quickly but for reasons that do not quite answer the issue raised; the suggestion taken from Eve in that debate, ratified by Adam's judgment though reluctantly, and supported by his own suggestion, the guiding model of domestic freedom ("thy stay, not free, absents thee more"). By cultivating delay and all the honorable devices of literary reticence, Milton has managed to create a pattern of "foreknowledge" without overt "influence," in which the suggestions do not bind but move toward the conclusion without violating the state of innocence. No suggestions overstep the fixed and restricted boundaries or begin an action that may be thought irreversible. The massive structure of intricately balanced delay both increases the weight of narrative inevitability and argues the case for justice in showing that the end is not necessary until it happens.

Against the train of suggestion, some of it perilous but none of it "depraved" (except Eve's dream, and that chiefly in its intent, which requires a second stage), a large counter-apparatus of solid instruction, divinely inspired, is brought to bear. It informs the mind and prefers to stimulate the active judgment and choice of rational inference, and not to offer passively received suggestion. So is God's will. And also Plato's, Aristotle's, *et aliorum fidelium.*

Milton's major fictional strategy was to invent suggestions that would not coerce. He needed to create an indeterminate stage of action—where movement was brief and discontinuous, intimating the potentiality of conflict and failure in "shadowy types" imperiling "truth" and "spirit." (His free imitation of some features of typological "prophecy"—carefully separated from divine guidance—is one of his great narrative inventions.) The action of that stage is played against the relief provided by the background of the Satanic example, that expressive body of determinate postmortem evidence against which to measure alternatives. On the indeterminate stage of tentative trial, Milton could gradually translate divine "foreknowledge" into fictional inevitability by showing judgment and choice moving toward the confusion of active and passive in the service of a necessity created by the actors themselves. The betrayal of divine love symbolized by the pledge of obedience must be preceded by the betrayal of knowledge, which, though limited by innocence and the principles of freedom, is not disadvantaged. Only God's knowledge is not limited. The betrayal of knowledge needed a counterforce created by the actors themselves, which had to be built out of suggestions, progressing like an argument but not systematically binding, a kind of imagined chain of unconnected links that can by the actors' choice become real and fast. What was like an argument then becomes an argument, and the fabulous elements of the present story become a demonstration of the truth and justice of the original sacred story.

Milton locates the fabulous elements of suggestion in the shadowy areas of consciousness related to dream and waking dream. The most prominent example is the imposed deceit of Eve's dream. This drops a large suggestion but leaves it open, and acts as a kind of wedge that does not compel her of its own force but does apply an external pressure that may help separate her from Adam and may—one is invited to think, but without exact evidence—help turn her into an agent of the agent of evil. Some of the inconclusiveness in the destructive pattern is counterbalanced in the providential pattern, for though Adam is not deceived by Satan, Eve is, and his love for the woman deceived by Satan helps justify the mercy announced for those not depraved "by their own suggestion." Whatever may be said by justice against human love, human love is not a "suggestion."

The major suggestion for Adam is entirely of his own devising. It resembles the limited impulse to reject of his first waking dreams, and is a kind of imaginative perversion, on his own, with ironic echoes, of his first true experience in the shadowy area of consciousness:

> *whereat I waked, and found*
> *Before mine eyes all real, as the dream*
> *Had lively shadowed.*
> *(VIII, 309–11)*

When Adam tries out his candid fiction of what "inward thence" he feels in response to passion, he is developing a suggestion of his waking dreams, but the effort is more advanced and deliberate, and fully staged in a famous dimension of consciousness over which the poet presides as expert. Adam projects the dangers of imagination innocently latent in Eve's charming love song. The ambiguities in her simple concentration, attending to her responses in order to create, are far more prominent and dangerous in Adam's complex effort at mimesis. He needs to "act" in order to express, and he seems not quite in control of the illusory elements in his presentation. This latter, in conjunction with the acknowledgement of inner division and the transposing of what is felt into the language of intellectual values, expresses the shadowy existence of the counterforce, the suggestion which motivates him toward the betrayal of knowledge and then the betrayal of divine love. What is given its tentative shape here, and then dropped, anticipates the beginnings of tragic experience when he does not recognize the depth of his involvement in the scene he must act—but cannot "act"—in the debate of Book IX. And it anticipates with ironic variation the way Adam solves his problem at the fall—not manipulating but abandoning reason, and both reversing his previous "approval" of separation from Eve and suppressing the sense of inner division, by integrating himself entirely on the side of his "heart's desire."

From our present advantage of review it should be clear that the design Milton invents does not honor his avowed obligations by imposing rigidities on the art of the storyteller.

Some of the materials of the last books of the poem I have reserved for particular treatment in the final chapter, where I shall also consider the changed purposes of Milton's story and the altered relations of the poet to his materials. For the most part I now propose to be brief and in this, the third stage of the human story, will touch only on those matters which concern issues we have been following.

From one point of view Milton has disposed his materials into the descending movement that leads to the Flood and the generally ascending movement thereafter. There may be some advantage, though, in recognizing a possible tripartite division. The first begins when Adam *decides* to be ruined and acts out some of the mental symptoms of the fall in advance. A kind of grim "foreplay" of exhilarated release leads to the episode of lust and then to the shallow, inadequate, but vivid anger they express toward each other. Only after they are reconciled can the second movement begin, the long re-education of Adam supervised by Michael. The third section is brief: the marvelous coda of Adam's return to Eve and their departure.

In the judgment scene Adam quickly unravels the heroic love which impelled him to unite judgment and choice entirely on the side of his "heart's desire." The speech before his judge is a dismaying performance, which begins with a parody of choosing and gallantry, winds and ducks as if he were trying to alienate the reader as well as God, and insinuates that the fault was not only Eve's but the fact that she was "thy perfect gift." Finally, in the last three words he admits what he did. In contrast, Eve is nearly overwhelmed with shame and answers in one simple line: "The Serpent me beguiled and I did eat." For the moment the two figures exchange the proportions accorded their separate falls, and seem to have exchanged much of their characters, roles, and claims on the reader's sympathy.

After Adam witnesses the "growing miseries" of the external world, he unburdens himself in the longest (non-narrative) speech of the poem, and does so in ways that invite comparison with Satan's first soliloquy. The Satanic background, which has provided a means of showing potential similarities, Milton now turns, with characteristic economy, into a surface against which actual differences can be reflected. One crucial difference between Adam and Satan is that small thread of human honesty preserved when Adam decides to be ruined for love but refrains from producing a facile apparatus of intellectual justification. Though Adam in soliloquy draws the explicit comparison "To Satan only like, both crime and doom," the difference is that all evasions, all of the plunging "through mazes," lead him to his "own conviction," which he accepts.

He cannot solve his problems alone, in monologue, but if he cannot make a proper beginning he can refuse to go further in the direction he regrets having taken, and he can go back at least as far as the acceptance of his personal responsibility. The new limitations imposed on his thought contrast with the successful ease of his best reasoning in the state of innocence. But the monologue rediscovers and makes belatedly clear that neglected resource of reason, the capacity to say no. Adam's passionate pursuit of the argument and its fictions is one more example of Milton's composing an archetype—that of sincere arguing with God in a "complaint" which dramatizes a position with intense feeling, but does not draw back from exposing the sterility of the efforts and from convicting oneself. The anticipatory echoes of Isaiah and Job, necessary to the archetype, are also evidence of the sincerity in his frustration. So too is a diversionary exercise in legalistic thinking, a sign of thinness which is countered by the recognition of a rational principle of justice. One sure difference from Satan is that Adam honestly craves answers to his questions. When the limits of knowledge are admitted, the admission is not like the device of Satan's argumentative wrestling with Abdiel, a bravado uncovering in public which requires more subtle covering in private. Satan on the abyss turns away in solitude; Adam facing the worst he can think, which includes pity for his descendants, does not turn away though he can go no further by himself. He must, the poet knows, think worse yet before he can think better, and this will require the presence of another, the emissary from heaven. But first he needs the help of Eve.

The monologue is a preliminary step in the direction for

which the renewal of love between Adam and Eve is a crucial second step. When they are reconciled—at Eve's initiative (like the separation and fall, and reversing their roles in the first courtship)—several obstructions are removed. Love begins again, and its dialogue—not without the normal trial, and help, of wrong suggestion, Eve's counsel of continence or suicide. They forgive each other and begin the first movements of love toward charity, and toward the extensive needs of social love. Eve offers to take all the blame on herself in sacrifice, but Adam pities her and her lack of understanding. He declares that he "Would speed before thee, and be louder heard," that all the judgment fall on him—"If prayers / Could alter high decrees." Their answers re-enact their behavior at the fall, with corrections, and Adam shows that he can control a conscious fiction. They then *remember* the signs of pity in their judge, and they pray.

Though prevenient grace has perhaps already acted (or is about to act, we cannot be sure), it does not diminish the evidence of human initiative and worth. Heaven responds and the second creation of Adam begins. It is painstakingly and painfully thorough. As Adam's vision of the future unfolds, to the reader much of it is like a bad dream remembered. All the foreground mercifully kept at bay by the poet in his telling of the story now enters with the experience of evil. Most of the items are short and episodic, but time passes more slowly for the reader than for Adam. Finally the promise of the Redeemer is understood, and the unfolding of Providence; Adam can review the essential human lessons and return to Eve and the long moment of their departure.

In conclusion, one subject seems to require some detached comment. It is the subject of human love, which is magnified out of proportion to other values in the destructive pattern of the fall and its consequences, and is then moderated in the tempering process through which human equilibrium is regained, though transformed, in the last books of the poem.

"How can I live without thee?" This is a question raised after the answer has been given, and is in any case not the kind of question intended to introduce the reasoned weighing of alternatives. Milton's artistic judgment in making the attractive, self-divisive intensity of Adam's love the pivot of his fall is not altogether different from Shakespeare's wisdom in such matters. In the tragic heroes love is never one thing—as it almost is in Romeo. Love is also the great dissembler under which other human drives act out their ultimate aims, not without some undermining perversities and transfers that escape the control of the cunning which thinks it knows what it wants. If we compare Adam's temptation with the full course in temptation presented to Jesus in *Paradise Regained*, or the short course offered by Satan to Eve, we may observe that in these latter examples all the temptations invite the sense of personal aggrandizement in the acquisition of power under various guises. Adam's temptation, in spite of all the things that can be said against it, is to surrender power and everything else if he can keep from losing Eve, for however short a time. The difference cannot alter divine judgment but can support Adam's claim to mercy. The range of permissible discrimination is admittedly narrow, since Adam is not directly deceived by Satan, or by Eve exactly. Though the nature of his love does change by a process of suggestion for which he is responsible, the ultimate source of his love is part of God's providential will manifested in the dialogue between Adam and his Creator. Adam is deceived by an intricate collaboration of his own suggestions; Eve is deceived by Satan and involves Adam. By this reasoning Adam would therefore, like Eve, become eligible for mercy: first, because the turning point of the fall is not his own suggestion and, second, because he is untouched (until after his mental decision) by the standard perversities of temptation promising self-aggrandizement. The first of these depends to a considerable degree on the assertion of Providence distinguishing between the Satanic and the human cases. The second depends chiefly upon the more examinable arguments for justice presented by the fiction—the differences in motive between Satan and Adam, and the differences in their response to the disasters they bring down upon themselves. These fine points are not opposed in spirit to observing that Adam's fault lies within a traditional area of tragic responsibility and does not deprive Adam of the compensating supports of tragic dignity.

When Milton shows that loving not wisely but too well opens the gates to destructive transcendencies and degradations, he is employing an established intellectual apparatus—one that usually concentrates on explaining effects and assumes that the causes are not unlike what they produce. Since the effects can be seen to emerge with dreadful

clarity, and since they lend themselves to systematic order-
ing, such evidence generally satisfies minds interested in the
practical application of accepted knowledge. In dealing with
the consequences of the fall, Milton accepts established wisdom, as he must unless he is to undertake the invention of an
entirely new one which would turn the story in another direction—besides, of course, requiring him to abandon his
own judgment in these matters. On the other hand, Milton
has put unusual effort, with marked success, into showing
the genesis of this love story from the beginning. There is no
intellectual passivity on his part in the effort to reach and
express the nature of human love. The only limitations are
those of artistic and personal tact—which include honoring
the mystery at the core and not exceeding his own capacities
to know and imagine. We do not need to discover in him
secret messages to confirm post-romatic values, but we still
may observe, and attribute to his conscious judgment, an
indestructible dignity in Adam's choice. That choice violates
all of Adam's accepted obligations—for a mysterious feeling
sanctioned and celebrated as right, though not autonomous,
and though changed without his knowing when Eve changed.
The choice leads to disaster, and Adam must suffer through
the experience of destructive changes before he can recover
and begin to renew what was not lost. There are new conditions, but the fundamental rightness of human love remains.

In Milton the penalties are exacted with uncompromising
severity from the lesser good chosen, and the degrading aspects of human love are painfully displayed. He does not,
however, ruin love, or overclarify its stubborn complexities,
or reason or moralize away its mysterious power. The love
that was beautifully celebrated before the fall, and not wholly
overwhelmed in the general destruction that ensues, recovers
on its own and takes an essential place in the paradise within.

One of Milton's most expressive inventions is to relate the
discovery of human love to the revelation of the Son's sacri-
ficial love. Both emerge from dialogue, from the sanction of
pre-existence in God's will, which is learned through free,
individual initiative in reasoning. Like the reason which participates in these acts of secondary creation, the two loves
may be thought to differ but in degree, both love and reason
deriving from God's love, which expresses itself in acts of
primary creation. The Son's love for the mortal, though it
clearly fulfills what is expected of filial obedience, is

nevertheless carefully marked off in a formal articulation as a lesser good "above which only shone / Filial obedience." Adam, lamenting Eve's loss and about to lose himself, speaks a line that is problematical in some respects but not concerning the place of human love: he declares Eve to express what is "Holy, divine, good, amiable, or sweet." The sweetness at the very first sight that she "infused" into his heart, "unfelt before," resembles the "Sense of new joy ineffable diffused" in heaven at the revelation of the Son's love. The exact center, binding and balancing, is the "good," which, while it holds, unites Adam's joy in the experience of human love and his joy in the divine and the holy.[18]

V.

The Art of Presence

We now come directly to the subject which, though brought forward often, has not usually been considered apart from other issues. Nor shall I want to break entirely with such procedures; in this chapter, however, the poet is the main issue. I shall work from examples and groups of examples. My occasional speculations will not reflect upon the nature and existence of "presence" itself, which I quietly accept, not wishing to quarrel with the object of my observation. Though the design of my scaffolding, its interest for itself, and even excitement, might well be improved by some delicate dismantling, I prefer the work I can do from it.

In the replies to the prayer which ends Book X we may see the poet engaged in the problems of reconstituting a new order for Adam and Eve. The spirit of the intended prayer is described by Adam and then echoed in the same language by the narrator, whose act cannot but draw attention to itself. The prayer is not given, only its essential spirit and the true signs accompanying. In accord with the authoritative teaching of Psalm 51 and Romans viii:26, the prayer is to be understood as expressing in "a broken spirit" and "groanings" a sincerity beyond words. Its eloquence, we are made to understand, exceeds that of the prayer which took the form of a hymn of praise in Book V. The eloquence of the hymn is fully open to our inspection, attributed to Adam and Eve but provided by the poet. Now, though as dramatic poet he composes Adam's description of the intended prayer, he then repeats the description as narrator. I infer, but shall not discuss now, that the poet intends to identify himself—as religious man—with Adam and the penitential prayer.

136

Meanwhile, after the corresponding action in heaven which takes up some hundred lines of Book XI, we return to Paradise at dawn, one of the regular times of human prayer. We find Adam and Eve just ending and at once experiencing the sense of "Strength added from above, new hope . . . joy, but with fear yet linked." The unspoken words on earth initiate extensive speeches in heaven by the Son and by the Father, and an action that is to fill most of the last two books of the poem: everything takes place in a synchronized long moment of time, including the human sense that the prayer has been answered, including some of the complexity of the answer as well, the linking of fear with joy. The composition of time is masterly in concept and execution, signifying a firm thread of continuity between heaven and earth even in the midst of change and separation. As soon as Adam commences to speak, however, to express in "welcome words renewed" what he has been experiencing without words, the spell of the long moment begins to come apart. The different rhythm of human time is "renewed," and the human concept of the relations with heaven and time expresses the uncertain grasp of a character under stress. One may add that a flexible degree of separation between the character and his dramatic poet is also "renewed," for the words Adam now speaks are deliberately composed to express his mixed feelings: which the poet may share as fellow man, or produce with a sense of artistic sympathy, or even mercy, but not without the separation of judgment.

"Eve, easily may faith admit. . . ." The adverb is ominous, and its reverberations extend to God's pronouncements in Book III: "For man will . . . easily transgress"; "what hellish hate / So easily destroyed, and still destroys"; and extend to Adam's first speech in Book IV: "This one, this easy charge," "One easy prohibition." The verbal echoes revive our sense of Adam's original masculine nature as Milton conceived and presented it: in which the capacities for joy and optimism are fundamental, though they are subject, under trial, to rationalized transformations in which joy becomes pleasure and optimism a kind of careless, facile hopefulness. The fact that Adam's observations are formally correct does not prevent some suggestion of an over-prompt upsurge of hopefulness, a kind of glib flow of formulaic piety expressed in an absent-minded syntax: "Hard to belief may seem; yet this will prayer." The "correctness" continues when the return of peace brings back the memory that there was a promise concerning the "bruising" of their foe and that this implied a future:

> *Whence hail to thee,*
> *Eve rightly called mother of all mankind,*
> *Mother of all things living, since by thee*
> *Man is to live, and all things live for man.*
> *(XI, 158–61)*

The broadening of the optimism, fundamentally right but conceptually inadequate, is the deliberately flawed work of the poet projecting the psyche of his Adam in response to circumstances. The concept of character certainly expresses the judgment of the artist, visible in the immediate expression and what that signifies; the judgment, moreover, reflects Milton's own thoughts on the nature of man. To be emphatic and obvious: the account does not claim to have been accurately observed and recorded; it is imagined, to fit a story, but it issues from a deeply considered and believed judgment of human nature in its masculine character. The poet we may see in the poem at this point is the figure of himself Milton could hardly have concealed had he wished to: that of the author whose representation includes his judgment (the circumstances fictional, the values participating in a fiction but possessing a separate existence as well). The figure of the poet does not obtrude but still is present substantially, answerable to the literary and philosophical questions addressed first to the dramatized character who speaks, and through him to the "living intellect" who creates and guides.

In the response given Eve the poet again adjusts himself to character and situation, maintaining the same responsible distance behind his speaker. Eve's feeling of shame is more prominent; she thinks less and feels more, responding to the sense of "infinite" pardon in her judge without attempting any thoughts which might lessen or divert her sense of guilt, and she does not respond to Adam's lifting hopefulness. Adam's masculine nature is oriented toward time and is emphatically ratiocinative, for better and worse. Before the prayer, and with no inner assurance of further life, his mind raced ahead to apprehend practical remedies, including the use of fire. After having prayed, he quickly concludes, from his inner feeling and from his recollection of the prophecy, "that the bitterness of death / Is past, and we shall live." Even

without the distressing signs of nature that soon contradict
Adam's easy interpretation of renewal, the thin outward
spreading of his optimism becomes unmistakable when he
concludes: "and all things live for man." The dramatic effect
seems to combine judgment and pity. On the other hand,
Eve's mind is not actively directed toward time, and her feelings are vaguely general or centered on a restricted focus: the
morning, the field, the day's work. Her nature is chiefly
oriented toward place and her husband. Her speech ends on a
note of feeling that owes little to the support of thought:

> *What can be toilsome in these pleasant walks?*
> *Here let us live, though in fall'n state, content.*
> *(XI, 179–80)*

The temperamental basis of her self-deception is different
from Adam's, and she makes no effort to give her desire any
rational development. The dramatic effect subordinates
judgment almost completely in pathos.

These comments are not intended as a summation of their
individual and related natures, but only, from a single
perspective, to indicate the strength and clarity of the composition that presents them, which also includes their individual differences as these are varied by conflict and development. (In the present scene we may be reminded of
some earlier evidence of conflict presented by the suggestion
of transferred roles, as each takes over some of the other's
distinguishing differences. For example, in the struggle for
dominance in the separation scene Adam found himself playing a traditional woman's part—giving in while hoping that
submission and dependence would exert their due leverage
on the reassured partner, and would control from below what
could not be directed from above.) The full development of
the story works through the limits and possibilities of order
in the harmony of their original differences, and recreates a
new order in the concluding harmony.

Throughout we know that behind the narrator there is a
man with a personal history, which also enters the poem.
Scholarly critics may well differ on the extent to which the
personal is merely disguised (this last is a common feature
that some art shares with psychic disturbances and their pal-
liatives), and differ on the purpose and success of those deeper
transformations of the personal which are always difficult to
identify with some degree of assurance. In the kind of tes-

timony of the self which art conceals and reveals in various ways, Milton should, like all writers, be submitted to the best questioning one can muster. The man has put himself on record with a lifetime of labor, print and manuscript, public and private, from boyhood to old age, and the record has been studied, reported on, and debated for three centuries by a body of individual experts, friendly, hostile, judicious, but all volunteer experts personally motivated. The nature of that motivation may have a single cause but not effect. The man has always provoked energetic efforts, and his record has produced a vast parallel record, in which one can read another kind of history, in which the personal is merely disguised, along with its attachments to the representative anxieties and beliefs, the identifiable matrix of another age. In the more complex and imaginative experts we may also read a history of deeper transformations of the personal—made available to us by our own skills in reading, by the techniques, urgencies, and insights inspired by our training in another age, and perhaps by our personal experience with disguises and transformations.

To return to the source: Milton the poet does seem to register high confidence in the art of self-expression, and does appear to be sublimely at ease with how he does what he is doing—at ease with the subtleties on and under the surface, with the narrative inventions and control, with the characterizing freedom of individual expression created to satisfy particular circumstances and conceptual aims. These are, whatever their ultimate source and process of differentiation, most clearly recognizable as attributes of the poet in his task, which is not without mysteries. Our own skills are justifiably more confident in detecting over-confidence and simulated ease which betray themselves by the cracks and strains that develop under our intense scrutiny of the words which turn purpose into accomplishment.

In his formal statements Milton admits no separation between the poet and the poem, between the birthright and the merit in the good life of a man who is an inspired poet composing a poem. In his own practice, however, he demonstrates a solid professional awareness of the special nature and demands of poetic merit. The "life beyond life" which he is treasuring up in this poem cannot be achieved without risk, devotion, skill, inspiration, and judgment (which must anticipate and supervise thousands of separate decisions); nor achieved without the nourishing pleasure he takes in the performance itself, in its inventions and coherence, in its constant need to solve present and distant problems. He must marshal his knowledge and foreknowledge and create while responding to the immediate opportunities of his fiction—an adventure from which he may learn what he could not previously have known; and if he is himself satisfied, he must find the expression that will satisfy others, endowing the particularities with significant life and with an imaginative justice in accord with the providence of his larger structure.

As the man is behind the poet who is behind the character, we are on the other side, responding to the character, but deeply interested in the poet's aims and art, and enjoying that range of his and our correspondence. We have our own individual histories too, and since these both help and hinder our performance as readers, they encourage us to imagine that the poet's experience was not altogether different. The modern intellectual passion for detecting and explaining incomplete transfers between conscious intentions and the deeper motives and habits of human nature has its own apparatus of reasoned belief, to which few of the walking wounded may consider themselves wholly immune. A skeptical estimate of the evidence is nevertheless free to observe that an artist who conveys the sense of exceptional pleasure in a performance characterized by exceptional esthetic success makes a formidable patient. The gleanings of wisdom which can be obtained in his case are better suited to explain the causes of his limitations and partial failures than the nature and effects of his triumphs.

To return to the poem and to an example related to our previous one, though now the judgment of the poet is not visible as guide and will respond only to a different kind of questioning: the example is Adam's response to Raphael's lecture on astronomy. The speech is an important one, for it defines wisdom and sets up standards through Adam's own initiative. By recognizing and expressing the standards Adam submits himself to their judgment, and he will return to them again in acknowledgment at the end of the poem. Nothing said so far seems to raise questions resembling those in the last example, but this episode occurs when Adam is still innocent, and the poet's guiding presence must obey the accepted difficulties in dramatizing a character who is "Sufficient to have stood, though free to fall." The expressive hopefulness of Adam's response after his penitential prayer can draw upon the standard resources of dramatic language—standard but capable of brilliant subtlety and precision. Adam innocent cannot reveal, because he does not have, the kinds of split and layered consciousness a dramatic poet can compose in complex vertical structures. Though one can, from the perspective of proved failure, mount a cross-examination of Adam's speech, such games are so easy to play that they do not seem worthwhile, except under strict rules and with attention to collateral evidence.

Materials of comparison may be borrowed, with acknowledged diffidence, from Adam's speech following his prayer. His response then is encouraged by a train of symptoms: a vision, or a mental image of God listening, not declared very certainly, but followed by a sense of inner persuasion, the return of peace, and an effective memory. The return of peace also follows the prayer in Book V; in the speech following Raphael's lecture on astronomy there is a partial resemblance in that Adam began in doubt and after the lecture is "cleared of doubt." A modest point of similarity is in the feeling of release, which in the speech on wisdom, however, takes a more positive and individual turn: Adam declares himself with great confidence, expounding the inferences drawn from the lecture into general principles. The authorized pleasure he takes in the strength of his mind is noteworthy; if his release from doubt stirs doubt in our minds we can produce no immediate justification other than the eager promptness and the voluntary fullness of his statement, and some preceding intimations that Adam enjoys exercising intellectual language in ways that do not always convince us that he hears himself judiciously.

Within the present speech there is no clear evidence of self-deception, as in our previous example. Yet we do not have to wait long before our diffident questions become necessary ones. The very confidence of Adam's pronouncements makes his behavior in the disclosure of passion all the more threatening; being able to define wisdom does not, it is plain, guarantee its possession. Nothing in the nature of innocence prevents an excessive trust in one's command of issues, however authoritative the language of their exposition. Indeed, even the terms of the definition become questionable as we see Adam's fancy roving exotically about a subject "which before us lies in daily life." Adam's categorical distinction between useless knowing "at large of things remote" and being effectively wise "in things that most concern" is, to say the least, rather too sharply drawn—and by a character who does not understand all the implications of what he so confidently says. One authoritative standard to apply is this: the dialogue with God does demonstrate a full capacity to understand both the "remote" and the immediate. Though the climate of opinion in seventeenth-century England fostered a wisdom which emphasized the knowledge of human concerns, and some distrust of the excesses of abstraction, any fit reader ought to agree with Milton's God when He praises Adam's demonstration of self-knowledge. That is, surely, the better wisdom (of which a pre-Christian saint and master of dialogue will be the prophet)—embracing, as it does, the remote, the immediate, and effective relationship. If we have developed our line of questioning properly, without abusing the rules of the story we do have some reasonable grounds for observing a lack of self-knowledge both in Adam's definition of wisdom and in the confidence of his procedure.

The presence of the poet may be discerned in his inventing the speech, its immediate context, its place in the larger context—and in his effective detachment. At moments of moral crisis and decision his own concept of wisdom resembles Adam's, but without necessarily rejecting the larger Socratic foundation, and his own career is notable for its displays of intellectual confidence and expression. Nor did he have to look far for a source in attributing optimism to the essential masculine character; the depth and durability of his own are Miltonic. Nor have we reason to doubt that the man, Milton, approved the judicious reticence of the poet, letting his character speak freely and well, submitting to no questions not of his own making. It is true that the questions of our making require efforts to observe the rules and spirit of the story, but the poet is therefore no less responsible; his judgment is back of everything said and not said. His restraints are those of art, and they are not to be confused with evasiveness or vagueness. His decision is not to *add* any visible signs of self-deception to Adam's speech, but he can and does *withhold* qualities which in their absence are not invisible to the mind. He withholds the expression of easy, relaxed control; the expression of a confidence based less on rigid separations and exclusions than on balance and self-knowledge; and Milton does withhold from the emphatic conclusiveness of Adam's speech any sense of general authority deriving from the poem and the poet. Milton does not wish us to forget that the pride stimulated by remote knowledge is a problem for man—though not until after the fall. Adam, it turns out, is over-emphatic in rejecting what is of no immediate danger to him. He celebrates too soon the liberation

> *from intricacies, taught to live*
> *The easiest way, nor with perplexing thoughts*
> *To interrupt the sweet of life, from which*
> *God hath bid dwell far off all anxious cares.*
> *(VIII, 182–85)*

Unfallen as well as fallen man may be "too secure" in reasoning out a rejection, not understanding that assurance may be premature if it does not comprehend the difference between not having said anything wrong and not having said everything right.

The episode is an unmistakable crux in the exposition of intellectual innocence, the knowledge of good without evil. Adam has already indicated touches of embarrassed awkwardness over the awareness of what he does not know or would very much like to know. Now for the first time we have a sustained example which suggests that he has been feeling a general pressure, perhaps cumulative and not derived entirely from the immediate subject introduced. (The moment is emphatically punctuated by the elaborate departure of Eve.) The subject of knowledge is a central issue that the narrative must engage, and we have had many occasions to observe the poet turning the materials of knowledge into story. Insofar as he attempts to silence all philosophical arguments outstanding to date, or to answer in advance all the questions Adam's descendants will have learned how to ask, he does so as religious thinker—but one who seldom falters in his responsibility to persuade as a poet.

Let us pause briefly to consider how within the story the subject of knowledge contains and touches on some related problems. There are traditional difficulties in the relations between feeling and knowing happiness, difficulties which the poet is not obliged to solve once and for all. The last words of the angelic chorus which celebrates the creation are "thrice happy if they know / Their happiness, and persevere upright." These words anticipate a famous quotation from

Virgil into which the narrator has (previously) introduced an ominous note: "and O yet happiest if ye seek / No happier state, and know to know no more." Adam feels that he is happier than he knows, and Raphael does not withhold knowledge that may "Infer / Thee also happier," though he counsels a proper daily wisdom: "Think only what concerns thee and thy being." Of the subsequent forbidden knowledge one might well say that when Adam leaves the Garden he knows that he is happier than he feels. The poet, we may observe, goes out of his way to relate the problems of feeling and knowing happiness to problems of obedience and of love and of knowledge. He deliberately assigns to the perfect bliss of Adam and Eve a formal declaration that no further growth will be possible during the present stage of their existence, and this is intended as part of the trial of obedience.

Knowledge has limits but the limits are not all of one kind, are not exclusively related to the external or quantitative, or to the infinite or divine or "other." The limits also define (or reflect) human nature by postulating a moral wisdom in which proper knowledge has a reciprocal function and serves the good life. Of this last the forbidden tree is a master symbol. Love is different, without limits in reference to God (unlike knowledge), but nevertheless limited by the disciplines of direction and control. Love as mercy may shine first and last, but not without satisfying an intellectual middle ground. This ground in turn cannot be separable from the ultimate purposes of God. Such reasoning, though it is peripheral to Milton's main enterprise, seems to require recognizing the concept of the "hidden God" whose nature, as many have thought, is only in part manifested in Scripture, the order of the world, and the reasoned interpretations of the sages. That God exists rather in the commanding "nothingness" of deity, in the pregnant omissions of Scripture, and may be traced in the varied efforts of "negative theology," and in the long record of human compulsion to attempt thoughts of the unthinkable and of the inexpressible.

For the most part Milton's "great argument" clearly chooses not to enter such regions but nevertheless marks their borders and does not act as if what lies beyond is a barren abyss empty of meaning. One brief series of images may serve to illustrate a significant range of the poet's attitude and artistic method. The *reality* of what is unknown is affirmed by the state of ready anticipation which exists in heaven. When God proclaims his enigmatic sentence on mercy "first and last," the ambrosial fragrance that fills heaven *diffuses* in the angels "Sense of new joy ineffable." The moment resembles, but is not identical with, Adam's first emotion: "With fragrance and with joy my heart o'erflowed." In Adam this leads to the personal discovery of God and to the personal sense of feeling happier than he knows, one of the more comprehensible forms of the ineffable. A deliberately similar moment, again not identical, occurs at Adam's first sight of the newly created Eve:

> which from that time infused
> Sweetness into my heart, unfelt before,
> And into all things from her air inspired
> The spirit of love and amorous delight.
> *(VIII, 474–77)*

Here the revelation is clearly and literally personal, and the new joy is *infused,* a fragrance to Adam's heart. In a less clear movement the spirit of love and delight is, as it were, *diffused*—"into all things from her air inspired." The movement is fraught with authorized human joy, but also with the free potential of excess and misdirection. These last are neither sanctioned nor prohibited as the uniquely aroused feelings make an expressive effort to understand a happiness "unfelt before." The poet invents the ambiguity, the potential confusion of innocent hyperbolical rejoicing. His invention, we may reasonably infer, is not uninfluenced by his own foreknowledge. He neither praises nor censures nor warns. Like the Creator who is the effective cause and the witness of Adam's response, he remains silent. Joy is, in the proper order of things, the right response, and the angels who share a "Sense of new joy" also feel that they are happier than they know. They too will learn something further of "The spirit of love," a complex lesson but utterly unambiguous and neither *infused* nor *diffused*. In the Son's exemplary act of freedom they will witness how "Transfused on thee his ample Spirit rests," (III, 389) and they will witness knowledge acting as love and love as knowledge.

The next examples will study the significant presence of the poet as he guides the poem through episodes which are similar enough to give observable distinctions considerable weight. I shall begin with Milton's management of Satan's perspective in the Garden.

Satan's presence dominates our attention through the long opening part of Book IV, and it is from his point of view that we first enter the Garden. Though Satan is there as a threat, and to provide the narrative with a touch of postlapsarian experience, Milton manipulates the positioning of Satan in novel ways that contrast with the dramatic liberties that he possesses in speech, where he is allowed to pioneer some of the subtleties of self-expression we may then recognize in Adam. In the Garden Milton quietly slips the descriptions out from under Satan's personal gaze to be taken over by the narrative voice. At line 205 Satan views "with new wonder"—which is Milton's pretext for assuming the perspective and celebrating the beauty in ways that are not obliged to express what the fallen angel literally sees. That the nominal viewer is in the grip of renewed wonder provides an established artistic excuse for going beyond current verisimilitude; the "wonder" furnishes a kind of imaginative bridge intended chiefly to mark the place of crossing with some token indication of definiteness. Once we have crossed, the bridge has served its purpose, and a new order of verisimilitude will produce its own justification if it is convincing, and Milton is confidently on his own ground when he comes to the landscape of Paradise.

At line 285 we return to the nominal viewer and the place we started from: "where the Fiend / Saw undelighted all delight." It is certain that Satan has been imposed on, contemptuously called "the Fiend" and turned into the passive spectator of a description he shares with the reader. He does not see directly himself but is the victim, as it were, of a transport of wonder by means of which the poet manipulated him. The pretext is one that may derive from the open palm of rhetoric rather than the closed fist of logic, but its opening into simple sensuousness does not lack the subtle and the fine, and the general effect is desirable enough to claim its origin from "an universal insight into things." The villain occupies the center of the stage but he does not so much *see* as *witness* what exceeds his personal vision. We have him there as example and as personal threat, but he is momentarily "overawed," "bereaved" of his personality, "stupidly good," as when he first confronts the beauty of Eve.

To introduce Adam and Eve, Milton returns us to Satan:

> *where the Fiend*
> *Saw undelighted all delight, all kind*
> *Of living creatures new to sight and strange.*
> *(IV, 285–87)*

The present writer, as reader, was long puzzled by the perspective which seems to start from Satan's view but without transition is removed from his ken. This is what I now believe Milton to have done, with a bold simplicity of technical invention that can support considerable weight of meaning. The bridge of wonder, once used with traditional artistic license, is then on the second occasion given a more abrupt and radical treatment. We cross from Satan's view to the description of Adam and Eve over Satan's inert body, which is mentioned and dismissed without formal pretext. The presentation is entirely separated from Satan, and the new verse paragraph ("Two of far nobler shape erect and tall") begins with an independent sentence, but one initially so sparing in verbs that we do not realize its independence until we have become thoroughly involved in what we are seeing. By that time we are only seeing for ourselves and have forgotten Satan, left far behind, neither help nor hindrance. Sixty lines later "the serpent sly / Insinuating" appears for a moment, but only as one of the creatures enlivening the landscape of Paradise, between the elephant and the ruminating herds. Then we make a formal return to the other side of the non-bridge:

> *When Satan still in gaze, as first he stood,*
> *Scarce thus at length failed speech recovered sad.*
> *(IV, 356–57)*

This last, the limpest line in the poem, is no expression of wonder, but it is a bridge to the inner complications of the soliloquy which follows, and it does express the deeper sense of Satan's relationship to the description that his presence frames.

The soliloquy is part of the standard background which Satan provides, evoking the postlapsarian experience which the reader may not apply to the central characters from his own foreground of human history. Milton's brilliant invention in his placing of Satan during the description turns the Satanic background from its usual composition of movement, change, and symbolic consequences into a static background completely arrested while an important movement, the first sight of Adam and Eve, is furnished with a sacred place from which the profane must keep their distance. Later Satan will violate their bower and intrude "Squat like a toad, close at the ear of Eve." But during the description of Adam and Eve Satan's evil briefly enacts what the narrative voice declared to be the result of the war in heaven:

> *Driv'n back redounded as a flood on those*
> *From whom it sprung, impossible to mix*
> *With blessedness.*
>
> *(VII, 57–59)*

Indeed, the day that God created man Raphael was sent to double-check the gates of hell, lest an "eruption bold" should anger God at work and thus cause a mixing of "Destruction with Creation." (We do not know the source or authority of Raphael's report, but the general analogy would seem to be applicable.) As for Satan's character and its dynamic capacity to move, there is also the other side expressed in this episode, the passivity which (even under the aspect of compulsiveness) represents the negativeness of evil.

The first sight of the human pair is treated as a sacred moment, a moving image of goodness against a background that is treated as both profane and inert. The poet's presence in this episode is for the most part that of a standard detachment, arranging matters to accord with the purposes of his narrative. It seems worth observing, however, that his purposes are unusual enough to evoke a certain arbitrariness in the skills he employs. Satan has invaluable services to perform. He regards the landscape of innocence as anguished observer; he is the destined antagonist whose inner drama expresses both a particular, objective threat and a comprehensive exhibition of the nature of evil as it acts upon itself; he will initiate the action upon which the next third of the poem turns. For good narrative reasons Milton wants Satan present. Though the Antagonist is no honest guide to the Garden, Milton has nevertheless arranged it so that our first entrance coincides with Satan's. The poet's descriptive work will then be, as he well knows, more difficult and more interesting; neither he nor his readers will be allowed to steep themselves in an undisturbed eloquence of nostalgia. Besides, we should feel a kind of moral shock which will not dull our alertness as we recognize that our admission into the Garden is shared by company whom we should not have chosen to invite. The poet simply overrules our sense of personal propriety and takes a far larger view of what is fitting for the expression of imaginative truth. Yet for one long moment of his own creative work he does not seem to be satisfied by the normal privilege of control by degree of artistic detachment; in presenting the first sight of the human pair he wants for himself and for his readers, whose responsive presence the poet does not forget, a moment of sacred concentration into which the profane is not allowed to intrude.

In the last chapter we observed from the viewpoint of Milton's narrative procedures the actions of Book V that follow Eve's demonic dream. Domestic Adam offers a comforting interpretation; they pray an "unmeditated" hymn of praise and then turn to their work. Like the silent penitential prayer at the end of Book X, the work seems to have remarkable power of expression: Adam and Eve prune those fruit trees which are "over-woody" and threaten fruitless growth (like the illusions that Satan stimulates), and they wed the fruit-bearing vine to the elm. These two simple acts are a symbolic rejection of Satan's dreamwork and a return to their peaceful participation in the goodness of the waking world. At this point God beholds the couple with pity, or so the narrator informs us in passing; most of God's reported speech concerns practical instruction to Raphael.

What is most remarkable about the handling of the episode is the narrator's position, which is not characterized by his practiced form of detachment or reticence. The degree of his acceptance of authority is open to question and may even seem obscure. He states the pity from the narrative point of view and is then content to back away, allowing God's attitude to be interpreted by the directions to Raphael. On the other hand, he ventures to interpret the general import of God's speech, and like the Son seems to listen with particular attention to God's closing words:

> *this let him know,*
> *Lest wilfully transgressing he pretend*
> *Surprisal, unadmonished, unforewarned.*
> *(V, 243–45)*

The interpretation is that God in the aspect of "Eternal Father" has "fulfilled / All justice," and there is no attempt to soften God's final words, which without interpretation could

sound like matter put on record in order to confront the crim-
inal with the justice of judgment when that time should
come. The poet has, we may observe, elsewhere demonstrated how such "gracious" interpretations can be made—
by the Son, whose birthright and merit are equal to the office.
If, as it seems, the narrator wishes to give the subject of pity
minimal articulation in his own voice, and wishes to refrain
from interpreting God's words and actions in reference to pity
while volunteering to name and emphasize the reference to
justice, we may well ask why.

Pity is named as the bridge to God's actions. As a narrative
device pity resembles Satan's first viewing "with new wonder" the world of the Garden. Almost everything except the
device is different, for Satan's wonder is an excuse for presenting poetic beauties which eliminate and transcend his complex involvement in what he sees. God gives direct expression to what lies across the bridge of pity, but the ostensible
subject receives hardly more direct expression than Satan's
wonder. The poet takes over the task of expressing wonder,
and entirely for his own purposes, but it is clear that he does
not wish to undertake any clarifying exposition of what
God's pity means, and how it may resemble and differ from
human concepts. The reticence of the poet is extreme; from
the expression of God's pity he eliminates himself almost as
completely as he eliminates Satan from the expression of
wonder.

A careful awkwardness in the syntax marks the spot where
the narrative voice names pity and begins to withdraw, as if to
disclaim the attribution in any literal way of a motivating
cause to eternal omniscience: "Them thus employed
beheld / With pity heav'n's high King." One may probably
assume that the prayer as well as the gardening is included in
the notice God takes of their employment, though it is
difficult to distinguish sequence in a "thus" when the eternal
looks at events in local time. The case would seem to be one
in which *orare est laborare* and vice versa. No separate cogni-
zance is taken of prayer, though at the beginning of Book XI
the Son as intercessor presents and interprets human prayer
to the Father, and the distinction between prayer and work is
clearly drawn in the later expression—as part of the divine
program of advancing the works of pity after the fall. Not so in
Book V, and the Son is notably absent from the scene as the
narrator presents it.

The work of pruning and viticulture opposes, with precisely chosen terms, the work of Satan's dream. The prayer is less direct as a counterforce but deeper, implicitly pruning away the inessential and cultivating the fruitful. Both prayer and work are human acts of initiative presided over by the poet, though unobtrusively. The hymn of praise is grand in scale and execution, an archetype in which we recognize traditional wisdom and eloquence worthy of an authoritative first expression. We may also recognize that the poet is conscious of what he is doing, and that the speakers understand, even without historical perspective, the import of what they are doing. The work, however, is different. Adam and Eve cannot possibly understand the exact symbolic relationship between the answer of their pruning and viticulture and the intentions of the dream. The episode is small in scale but breathtaking in its perfection, and the narrator's presence behind the scene cannot, however quiet, be disguised. His intelligence and compassion are doing more than invent an act for his protagonists to perform; he is interceding, interpreting, mediating between human distress and divine pity; he is, one might say, implanting a kind of grace not in the official transcripts or appended comments: one may call it "narrative grace."

However unobtrusive, to human eyes, the act of the poet is very bold and in one respect seems to venture beyond the divine rules of freedom in countering Satan. For the work, the symbolism of which is not understood by the actors, touches the will; an external cause moves Adam and Eve to *oppose* Satan from within, without knowledge, without deliberate choice. When it is the narrator's turn to interpret God's speech, the Son still not having appeared, he can counter any imputed boldness in his previous action by proclaiming "All justice." But his voice is not the simple one that announced the return of peace and calm. The Son never interprets the Father, or intercedes (which always amounts to the same thing), without an elaborate apparatus of ritual to counter any possible shade of unaware presumption. The poet filling that office, though as invisibly as possible, maintains the silence of a true ghost writer. But in the difficult relation between pity and justice we may perhaps detect the poet's conscious presence in the unusual assignment of epithets. When it comes to mentioning pity, God's power and remoteness are emphasized; He is called "heav'n's high King," while the author of "All justice" is named "Eternal Father." The least one may say is that the prayer and the symbolic work, which the poet quietly creates without needing to stand up for observation, are different. These, being offered to God's pity, are free to develop their own beautiful appropriateness in a human voice unweighted by the impediment of speaking or interpreting God's remote language, which the poet cannot create unobtrusively.

The poet who takes the initiative for mediating between human distress and divine pity does not invoke any intervening support of established poetic, intellectual, or religious traditions. Without dialogue or circumspect ritual he "interprets" God's will. The moment is like no other in the poem—bold, brief, and touching one kind of extreme.

As the third and concluding example in the present series let us consider a less radical and more "literary" instance which illustrates an extreme of elaborate self-consciousness. As Adam raises the subject of astronomy with Raphael, a long transitional moment centers on Eve. She notices the studious look on her husband's face and rises from her "retired" seat to visit her "nursery" of fruits and flowers. The moment is carefully constructed and placed. It begins with the brief signal of Adam's appearance and Eve's observation, and it ends with a ceremonious praise of Eve's beauty in departure, a beauty praised to the same effect as she first rises from her seat. She has been, for many hundreds of lines, out of sight and mind. Not now, as she leaves under full masculine attention, not least of all the poet's:

> *With goddess-like demeanor forth she went;*
> *Not unattended, for on her as queen*
> *A pomp of winning Graces waited still,*
> *And from about her shot darts of desire*
> *Into all eyes to wish her still in sight.*
> *(VIII, 59–63)*

And then Raphael turns to Adam and immediately picks up the question so charmingly interrupted.

The grace of her rising "won who saw to wish her stay," and her leaving strikes "all eyes to wish her still in sight." On the one side there is an expressive intensity, on the other a silent message of brevity. A decorative flourish, highly stylized, enlarges her grace to a "pomp" of graces armed, and brings a potential world of spectators to enjoy the lingering moment with Adam and Raphael. The poet leans into his task with enthusiasm, as if the action were invented to create the poetic opportunity for celebration. Nor does he neglect the response waiting in Eve's "nursery," which has not been visited since Book V:

> they at her coming sprung,
> And touched by her fair tendance gladlier grew.
> *(VIII, 46–47)*

And the remote possibility that Eve's action may be misinterpreted by a potential world of spectators, little accustomed to such privileged viewing, requires a correction in advance. The correction is at first carefully encrusted with negatives and then suggests an explanatory reason, with side-flourishes and with syntactical reservations which are exquisitely tactful and elusive, after which a direct rhetorical question seems to put everything under the retrospective cover of simple praise:

> Yet went she not as not with such discourse
> Delighted, or not capable her ear
> Of what was high: such pleasure she reserved,
> Adam relating, she sole auditress;
> Her husband the relater she preferred
> Before the Angel, and of him to ask
> Chose rather; he, she knew, would intermix
> Grateful digressions, and solve high dispute
> With conjugal caresses; from his lip
> Not words alone pleased her. O when meet now
> Such pairs, in love and mutual honor joined?
> *(VIII, 48–58)*

Later that afternoon, as time was then, about five hundred lines later, we can perceive from our "retired" seat some further "studious thoughts" which motivated Eve's departure and made a ceremony of her exit. She becomes, not present, the uninhibited main subject of an intense discussion. This, the last turn of what has been a leisurely narrative, could not gain its particular intensity, perfectly timed and placed, if there were not an unbroken amplitude of preparation and an undisturbed evenness of tempo out of which the surprising moment can evolve. One is well occupied at Eve's departure. Looking back, after a whole week silently elapses between Books VIII and IX, one recognizes that her necessary exit occurs at the one opportune time. From the perspective of Book

IX one clear, small fact does emerge: the precedent of Eve's own easy acceptance of occasional solitude. Being innocent, though beautiful, she no doubt was unaware of her effect on husband and angel (and on poet and reader) as she left. She might, however, have observed that her absence did not abbreviate a conversation which continued until "shut of evening flow'rs."

How much stress is it reasonable to put on her attitude toward solitude, or on her apparent motive suggested by the poet, her preferring to "reserve" her pleasure by waiting until she can be "sole auditress" of her husband? In estimating these matters we need to watch as well as listen to the narrator. He mounts an extravagant display which in degree of virtuosity, if not in substance, cannot seem quite native to Paradise ere fallen. When the master of language expresses himself so fully, the high credit he has acquired thus far does not encourage us to accept a literal or a naive identification of the poet with everything said. If our choice lies between assuming a sincerely naive or a sincerely complex poet, at the present juncture we should not hesitate long, and it will seem reasonable to recognize that the fullness of expression is juxtaposed in particular ways with unacknowledged brevities and omissions. No direct articulation points to the contrast between the protracted ceremony of Eve's departure and the immediate resumption of the masculine talk:

> *And Raphael now to Adam's doubt proposed*
> *Benevolent and facile thus replied.*
> (*VIII, 64–65*)

We are not invited to speculate over what Adam will tell Eve when the angel goes, and where in the account the "Grateful digressions"—or omissions—will come. But we cannot miss, and the narrator knows we cannot, the difference between his own elaborations of Eve's suggested motive and the personal ring of her first speech in Book IX. There she seems to have satisfied for the moment her pleasure in being "sole auditress," and she has some "first thoughts" of her own for Adam to hear.[1] "From his lip" neither "smiles" nor "Casual discourse" will now please her. Nor should we miss there the novelty of Adam's realization that it is dangerous for Eve to be unaccompanied in the Garden. Neither he nor Raphael gave the slightest evidence of concern as they admiringly watched her leave.

I do not think that we have a naive narrator, and if he is "unreliable," he is not playing a role that the experience of the reader can readily translate into moral or other instruction. Behind the poet's display John Milton stood or sat "retired," pronouncing his *r*'s with customary emphasis, enjoying the strain of the narrative need to protest too much and giving the fit reader fair warning that excess did not guarantee the expression of the whole truth. Participating in the gracefully awkward scene as they do, the Adam who can smile "with superior love" and the masculine angel (with his measured appreciation of Eve) may both be willing to accept the poetic ceremony and the suggested motive for her leaving. The experienced reader is in a better position to take note and wait. To the extent that the poet participates in the story at this point, emulating the ready hopefulness which is a sign of original masculine nature, the chief benefit accrues to the story, and one must then admit a certain inconsistency in, or mark an extreme range of, the narrator's role.

If we conclude that there was a lapse in his foreknowledge, and no deliberate withholding of narrative purpose, and that only later he, like us, discovered that the story needed Eve's departure at this particular time, we must then put him into the story—and on a plane more like than unlike that of the other actors, and not like Adam and Eve protected from our judgment by their state of innocence. The literary hypothesis will then quickly turn into a psychological one, with "no narrow frith" to cross and with no vehicle other than that of a psychological fiction offering a deeper and truer story than the one we think we have been reading. It seems to me preferable to assume that Milton did involve the narrator—for special but limited purposes. The poet's hopeful business in managing the scene is partly misleading, but not without signs to warn us that he speaks with less than full and precise authority here—at least in presuming to explain the woman. We do not doubt his accuracy in describing masculine response, the excesses and brevities of which are not without symbolic value if we wish to immerse ourselves in the contemplation of the fall as unique mystery. The scene is a brief, memorable episode of articulate embarrassment, turned inward and outward in strange ways, and bearing some resemblance to the revelation of angelic sex when Raphael acted as narrator.

The poet who interpreted God's pity was as inconspicuous as possible; here he is conspicuous, deliberately I think, and for the sake of the story, which needs another voice at this point. One may mark an opposite extreme when the poet signals an identification with the penitent Adam at the end of Book X and then for much of the last two books withdraws from his inventive art of presence.

If there were an invocation for Book XI Milton might have been forced to admit the purpose of changing his notes from tragic. He would not, I think, have had an appropriate literary term available, and "comic" in the traditional Dantean sense would have been misleading. Adam, having in his first life represented ideal human nature in a tragic perspective, is to be regenerated as the first Christian, and submitted to an intense education distantly resembling a progress through hell and purgatory before entering the world. There are marked changes in the conduct of the last two books, and therefore in the poet's relations to his material. It is to the latter that I shall direct most of my attention.

As the human prayers rise to heaven in sighs "Unutterable" without divine help, we learn from the narrator that "Prevenient grace" has acted first and started the process of regeneration. Milton the theologian has now begun to chart the technical steps leading through repentance to faith. But Milton the narrative poet has left the timing ambiguous, or at least indefinite, and has left open in their presentation, as if uninfluenced from above, those free acts of individual initiative that led, from the reasoned acceptance of responsibility by Adam and the spontaneous plea for forgiveness by Eve, to their reconciliation and renewal in love. The conjunction of their two human natures is beautifully convincing and expresses the effective divine love which first created them. The poet's work in expressing that love is delicate in tact but firm and unyielding.

At the beginning of Book XI, however, the narrative poet seems to have lost some of the advantage he articulated with relief in the invocation to Book VII: he does not seem to be quite "Standing on earth . . . More safe I sing with mortal voice, unchanged." The illustrative myth of Deucalion, borrowed and qualified with less than usual grace, is not improved when—against his better practice—he invents a decorative myth to describe the ritualistic progress of the prayers. The Son then takes over in his role as priestly mediator:

> *See, Father, what first-fruits on earth*
> *are sprung*
> *From thy implanted grace in man, these sighs*
> *And prayers, which in this golden censer, mixed*
> *With incense, I thy priest before thee bring,*
> *Fruits of more pleasing savor, from thy seed*
> *Sown with contrition in his heart, than those*
> *Which, his own hand manuring, all the trees*
> *Of Paradise could have produced, ere fall'n*
> *From innocence. Now therefore bend thine ear*
> *To supplication, hear his signs though mute;*
> *Unskilful with what words to pray, let me*
> *Interpret for him, me his advocate*
> *And propitiation; all his works on me,*
> *Good or not good ingraft; my merit those*
> *Shall perfect, and for these my death shall pay.*
> *Accept me, and in me from these receive*
> *The smell of peace toward mankind; let him live*
> *Before thee reconciled, at least his days*
> *Numbered, though sad, till death, his doom (which I*
> *To mitigate thus plead, not to reverse),*
> *To better life shall yield him, where with me*
> *All my redeemed may dwell in joy and bliss,*
> *Made one with me as I with thee am one.*
>   *(XI, 22–44)*

The passage seems overwrought, including the preliminary lines not quoted above, as if Milton suddenly is trying too hard, composing a first ritual that ought to be simpler, and that suffers unduly from comparison with the triumphs of Book III. One may perhaps attribute the self-consciousness and sense of strain to Milton's writing on a subject far less congenial to him than the rejected subject of wars and havoc. No doubt he is more at ease in an "unmeditated" hymn of praise, or in imagining song and dance in heaven, or in destroying the symbols of idolatry, including the Garden as a sacred place, than in producing the rites of a priestly archetype. But his professional skills have been equal to other tasks not always congenial. He chose the subject, furthermore, and gave it greater emphasis than might have been necessary if he were not moving into a new and different stage of the poem. The re-education of Adam is to be conducted under the rules of theology, and though Milton does not destroy all of Adam's past, he is grimly methodical and severe in laying the grounds for the new future. At least one practical narrative justification may be adduced: Adam and Eve are already entertaining thoughts of patching together their old life, and we are about to hear Adam's facile optimism in the speech, "Eve, easily may faith admit." The Son presents a formal veto in the suggestive declaration that the new life is already better and that the fruits of contrition are more pleasing to God than

> his own hand manuring, all the trees
> Of Paradise could have produced, ere fall'n
> From innocence.

Though the judgment is in part mitigated by a standard ritual of expression, contrasting man's purpose and God's, God's work in contrition and man's in gardening, the statement is painful, nevertheless, in its prompt dismissal of man's work, innocence, and the Garden itself—as if these had been merely second best all the time. And so perhaps they have been, from the perspective of Providence now being abruptly interposed. For we are now into the part of the poem which has the task of asserting Providence, and the poetic methods cannot be the same as those required to "justify the ways of God to men." The latter have produced the argument of a human story; the last two books deploy their materials differently. This is not to deny that the human responses are at the center and are carefully arranged to permit some awful shocks, gradual recuperation, suspense, growth, and ordered recovery. The action at the center continues the human story, but the great bulk of the action concerns the materials of scriptural history; the arguments depend on the assertions and rational development of doctrines which owe very little to the kinds of persuasiveness native to the freer air of a serious fiction. Even great writers may not exceed their "active spheres assigned."

These are not unfamiliar objections to the last two books of the poem, and they can in part be countered by critical emphasis on the larger issues of Milton's structural intentions and on his masterly control of many details. He is determined to express the full cost of tragic experience and to do justice to his vision of man's effective hope by not imposing the easy solutions of optimistic lyricism. Adam does undergo a full and convincing progress through a relentless course of expiation, with believable faltering and lapses, and a gradual recovery of confidence in his own faculties. The characteristic proof is that he participates with growing initiative and independence of judgment in the dialogue with Michael. This is part of the story Milton carries through with unimpaired mastery of his resources, both as narrative artist and as prophet of the unbroken continuities in human life.

My accepted commitment to the human story and the poet's relations to it may justify dwelling on the nature of difficulties over which he does not triumph to the same degree or in ways he has prepared us to expect. There *are* moments of intense human interest, such as Eve's pathetic anguish at the news that they must leave Paradise. As often, Adam sounds pallid in comparison but shows himself to be deeper and more durable. Such moments, however, give the poet back the materials of his old story; it is the new story and its methods which reveal a different poet.

To begin with, Michael (as did Raphael before him) takes over most of the narrative task, interpreting his assignment from God with marked freedom and latitude. The image and presence of the poet which Milton has deliberately created and involved in much of the poem for the most part now recedes. (The poet who turned over the task of narration to Raphael did so to enlarge the imaginative discourse and the authority of its great scope and variety; no effect of contraction is felt by the choice of Raphael as narrator.) The poet does emerge rather prominently to conduct the preliminary survey of the kingdoms of the world and to attend the clearing of Adam's eyes "to nobler sights." After that, his formal task is to mark transitions and, often in a toneless voice, to give Adam's responses. In the larger task of presenting visions, Michael is the presumed author—though Michael at certain strong moments wisely chooses to sound like Milton. Once, briefly, the poet speaks in his own human voice, when Adam responds as a father at the loss of all his children in the Flood: "How didst thou grieve then, Adam, to behold."

What is almost entirely missing until the end of Book XII is that sense of presence, characteristically aloof and enjoying its exercise of strength, skill, and degrees of visibility. There are no calculated interruptions, no moments of engaging reticence, no art of encouraging the reader to anticipate the poet and rewarding such failures, no art of surprise. The choices representing the mastered life of the poet present in the poem are not the complex ones which may hope to unite the fabulous and the demonstrative. The story does not admit the inventions of fable and is presided over by the Muse of history and (the meaning not the name) that of doctrine. The constant pressure to keep the foreground of fallen experience from acting as general background of the human story—a pressure in which the presence of the poet is variously felt— simply disappears as that foreground becomes the matter of the story. The sense of the poet's detachment as a valid symbol of his personal equilibrium has no further office to perform. He is no longer felt to be on trial himself, responsible for his privilege of narrative foreknowledge, for his own suggestions, and for the judging and choosing on which the truth of the story depends. One may attribute these differences to the accepted guidance of theological reasoning, which authorizes the asserting of Providence.

The critic smartly listing the losses cannot expect to gain much satisfaction from his exercise of literary judgment, and he may well feel that the principles of art have been deliberately violated in deference to higher values. We may perhaps mark the penitential identification with Adam at the end of Book X as the point where Milton gives up the privilege of his position, which he has been brilliantly justifying, to share in the general calamity and to begin the sober rebuilding from a position of less detachment and individual flexibility. There are some signs that may lend credence to the suggestion. There is also, of course, the essential pattern of his Christian belief which is committed to the proposition that, in spite of all to be said on the other side, the world saved must be better than the world lost. One may respect the proposition without subscribing to it. One may also observe what the belief does to the poetry, and observe the nature of the burden it imposes on the poet. Yet, whatever the final assessment and the critical explanations offered, Milton is not likely to be denied power and greatness of voice in speaking for the world lost.

In accord with the providential values which events are beginning to bring forward, the wordless penitential prayer has to be better than the hymn of praise in Book V, though the latter is one of the glories of the poem, anonymously composed by the poet for Adam and Eve. Adam penitent initiates still another human experience in its authoritative first occurrence. Unlike most of the previous examples, however, this experience cannot be registered within the confines of a scene or passage, with all the artistic advantages of intense realization in the focused clarity of a sustained moment. The repentance is transitional and emergent, evolving from a ruin providentially foreseen, an archetype in the process of establishing itself as an exemplary model for life outside the Garden, in effect reaching out beyond the limits of the story. What is tentative in Adam's experience, including the first discovery of obstructions, errors, and relapses, is in the spirit of a fictional discourse. On the other hand, the protracted length and difficulty of the stage, and the carefully prescribed steps leading to faith, clearly correspond to traditional wisdom on the subject, however brought up to date by the judgment of an individual redaction. Something in the apparent identity of writer and man does not work to the benefit of the story. As Adam's fall affected the world of nature, the poet's penitential identification with Adam affects the world created by the poem.

In retrospect, the dignity of work in the Garden receives a peremptory devaluation in the Son's praising the first fruits of contrition "in this golden censer mixed / With incense." These fruits are "of more pleasing savor"

> than those
> *Which, his own hand manuring, all the trees*
> *Of Paradise could have produced, ere fall'n*
> *From innocence.*

Whatever may be said in justification of the doctrine, the sudden casualness of its mention creates a number of shock waves. One may not wish to debate God's privilege to reduce the importance of the love expressed in His first creation, but it was a novelty of the poet's own judgment and choice that in its emphasis gave distinct value to human work in the Garden. The symbol was a vulnerable one and it required careful poetic work to make it valid. At least once the poet succeeded in raising the hands at work into a sacrament of his own devising: after their purgative hymn of praise Adam and Eve pruned the "pampered boughs" of fruit trees and married the vine to the elm, both countering the purposes of the demonic dream and rejoining the fruitful works of God's "goodness beyond thought." And God beheld them with pity.

The system of truth compiled by doctrine requires us to prefer the fruits of contrition to the work and prayer of innocence. In managing its own business the poem introduces a further extension. We are required to prefer, as a by-product of the new order, the elaborations of ritualistic mediation to the simple, unmediated encounters of man and God—in spite of the sustained eloquence of the latter and the abrupt arbitrariness of the former. Neither doctrine nor reason, however, requires us to admire the transposition of Psalm 51 from a human offering to God, stumbling in praise and eloquent in grief, into a divine expression of glad praise for the broken spirit. The indecorum, if I do not misinterpret and exaggerate, would seem to reflect the poet's unusual sense of strain in moving to the new order of rejection and preference.

These matters, it should be plain, cannot be argued as if uninfluenced by convictions—or "taste" at least, both religious and literary. I acknowledge my awareness of counterarguments which satisfy others. Minds no doubt better regulated than my own appear to accept with no reservations the appropriateness of the first ritual by the priestly mediator. And some critical readers, noting the deliberate development of the imagery of growth from "implanted" to "ingraft," regard the speech as largely successful in accomplishing a difficult task.[2]

On the other side, however, there are the standards which, if not misconstrued, the poem has created and sustained. These have so convinced me of their rightness that I resist putting them aside, and I find myself not quite persuaded that the new conditions justify the new style of expression. We seem to be asked to accept earnest and straightforward artifice presented with sincere effort, and with no visible reservations by speaker or poet, an elaborate speech immune to the kinds of scrutiny and judgment which Milton has been requiring of his readers. Does the poet persuade us by his own narrative description?—

> To heav'n their prayers
> Flew up, nor missed the way, by envious winds
> Blown vagabond or frustrate: in they passed
> Dimensionless through heav'nly doors; then clad
> With incense, where the golden altar fumed,
> By their great Intercessor, came in sight
> Before the Father's throne.
> (XI, 14–20)

When the Son mixes prayers with incense to recommend their "pleasing savor" and to gain from God "The smell of peace toward mankind," the figurative expression does not compare well with the echoes it awakens. We remember the "ambrosial fragrance" that in God's attending angels "Sense of new joy ineffable diffused," and Adam's heart overflowing "With fragrance and with joy," and the sweetness "infused" at the first appearance of Eve, and the morning light which turns the earth into a "great altar" breathing the silent praise of fragrance to the Creator.

These examples all suggest the sacramental, and they use figurative language in a similar way. In the *Christian Doctrine* Milton speaks of "this figure of speech in the sacraments, where the relationship between the symbol and the thing symbolized is very close. . . ." Thus did "biblical writers" employ the figure, "to denote the close relationship . . . and also to show that these spiritual matters were sealed with absolute certainty. Thus the same form of speech is used in other instances where the absolute certainty of a thing is to be expressed. . . ." If we borrow a limited point of view from the *Christian Doctrine*, we may interpret the image of fragrance as a figure intended to emphasize both "close relationship" and "absolute certainty." The point of view is limited, however, and overlooks the Protestant theologian's interest in reducing the multiplication of sacraments; and also overlooks Milton's normal distaste toward emphasis on the "outward sign," an emphasis generally associated with Roman Catholicism but not entirely avoided in the Son's speech.[3]

To conclude this part of the discussion let us consider some additional comparison from within the poem. In a beautiful set piece Adam responds to Eve's affectionate leaning against him:

> half her swelling breast
> Naked met his under the flowing gold
> Of her loose tresses hid. He in delight
> Both of her beauty and submissive charms
> Smiled with superior love, as Jupiter
> On Juno smiles, when he impregns the clouds
> That shed May flowers.
> (IV, 495–501)

The moment is a memorable one, a collection of forces held together in the painter's marvel of clarity, all surfaces realized in the privilege of their arrested moment, and the flow of time held fast and felt as a pressure balanced from within and suspended from without. The decorative myth is unusual but brief, and if we are inclined to question its artifice or the full implications of "superior love," we must do so against the energetic pressure of Satan's immediate interruption. The poet is free to indulge his and our pleasure. He does not have to "justify" anything beyond the compass of a beautiful moment of lovers embracing.

But consider another example in which an illustrative myth is produced as an official truth complete and as if literal through and through. In Book III the angelic choir hymns the Father with concentrated power, the expressive substance of which can be developed only by an exemplary action of light and a related temporal movement. Next the choir celebrates the Son (and the Father through the Son) in a song that reviews major events in heaven: the creation, the rebellion and victory (at some length), and the revelation concerning man, which has just occurred. Man is, in heavenly time, already fallen by "malice," but the vengeance executed upon angelic foes by the Son does not, will not fall upon man:

> *Not so on man; him through their malice fall'n,*
> *Father of mercy and grace, thou didst not doom*
> *So strictly, but much more to pity incline.*
> *No sooner did thy dear and only Son*
> *Perceive thee purposed not to doom frail man*
> *So strictly, but much more to pity inclined,*
> *He to appease thy wrath, and end the strife*
> *Of mercy and justice in thy face discerned,*
> *Regardless of the bliss wherein he sat*
> *Second to thee, offered himself to die*
> *For man's offense.*
>
> *(III, 400–10)*

The reported "strife" in God's face is a myth invented for the occasion, a residue perhaps from medieval debates of the four daughters of God. If we find it jarring (as I do) we cannot attribute it to angelic enthusiasm with which the poet does not identify himself. He has, with commanding technique, mingled himself in the chorus by joining the "sacred song" to the narrative voice without transition. No stimulating reticence is intended, no projection of partial or faulty knowledge that we may see again from a subsequent perspective. Instead, the myth which undertakes to explain a mystery of God's nature makes its brief punctuation and is abandoned.

Yet the assertion is too prominent, and the literal detail too insistent, for a merely decorative piece of imagination—like Jupiter smiling on Juno. Though brief, the moment is not designed to be forgotten, which may perhaps be said of Raphael's token myth on the possibility of God's wrath causing Him to mix "Destruction with Creation." That is, though fascinating, not a clearly authorized explanation; it is lightly dropped and moved away from, and the narrator's own connection is kept remote.

One would feel more comfortable perhaps if the angels were overextending themselves, fabling and erring, but the poet has registered his own presence fully, though in putting himself into the story at this point he is competing against the far better story which he has drawn. The myth would seem to challenge the authority of the dialogue in heaven, and would present us with a Son whose "merit" seems in part prudential. Even *time,* in a small dimension Milton deliberately and successfully excludes from considerations of heaven, creeps in: the Son is praised for reflecting a rapid assessment of the Father's inclination: "No sooner did . . . ." Even the factuality of the asserted report is troubling, given the celebrated invisibility of God. If God is visible only in the "conspicuous count'nance" of the Son, the myth has a deceptive plainness, and the speakers are either inventing wholly or their complex vision has the benefit of a technical mystery which might at least have been mentioned.

Nor does the solemn iteration serve to increase the authority of the report:

> thou didst not doom
> So strictly, but much more to pity incline.
> . . . .
> not to doom frail man
> So strictly, but much more to pity inclined.

Though the whole poem is a vast organization of echoes, the choir seems to be borrowing for special purposes a form of iteration that has already been recorded as the style of divine usage:

> To pray, repent, and bring obedience due.
> To prayer, repentance, and obedience due.
> (III, 190–91)

Once, in a solemn moment, at the end of Book X (1086–1104), the poet will emulate the expressive device and repeat in the narrative voice the words he has put into Adam's mouth. The moment is crucial. The poet is not asserting, like God, nor asserting like the choir of which he is a part; he seems instead to be acknowledging, or even more, pledging an identification with the penitent Adam. The moment is the poet's own deepest expression of personal humility in the poem, lacking, as it does, that customary Miltonic upswing of hope after the worst has been said. The moment marks an important transition for the poem and for the role of the poet, marking the kind of change that has usually invoked the Muse and produced a personal statement of great poetic force, breadth, and elevation. The poet repeating the words of the penitent Adam is accepting a "better fortitude" than patience for the most difficult subject of his "heroic song."

To return to the angelic choir of Book III and the poet's presence fully committed. If I do not misconstrue, the episode fails in its intention and creates an unwanted side-effect rare in Milton's rhetoric: it increases the visibility of the effort without increasing or redirecting the significance. The best I can say of the passage and of the poet's presence is that Milton made an unusual but brief mistake.

Before we return to the main track, I should like to approach the opening of Book XI from another direction. In a peripheral argument supporting man's freedom and a distinction between God's foreknowledge and His decrees, Milton advances in his *Christian Doctrine* the thought that "the idea of certain things or events might come to God from some other source. Since God has decreed from eternity that man should have free will to enable him either to fall or not to fall, the idea of that evil event, the fall, was clearly present in God from some other source: everyone admits this."[4] There is no formal mention of such in *Paradise Lost*: man is "deceived" and the Satanic host fall "by their own suggestion." But the first announcement of the fall is made as God watches Satan headed toward earth and man, intending to try

> *If him by force he can destroy, or worse,*
> *By some false guile pervert; and shall pervert;*
> *For man will hearken to his glozing lies.*
> *(III, 91–93)*

We seem to be given some opportunity to witness foreknowledge spontaneously expressing prediction as an "appointed season" of time looms into view, the conjunction of Satan and Adam. If we take up the speculative assertion of *Christian Doctrine,* we may perhaps regard the present occasion as an example of "some other source" introducing the idea of a specific event into the eternal decree concerning freedom. The poem, however, does not argue the point but seems more interested in staging the revelation of Providence. (The major purpose of the scene is, of course, to present an exemplary act of freedom, which our concentration on other details is not intended to deny or obscure.)

When the Son takes up the task of interpreting the Father's intentions, the answer is that he has expressed the truth of what the "eternal purpose has decreed"—that mercy "first and last shall brightest shine." When the Son then volunteers to sacrifice himself for man, the Father, in an extraordinary act, assumes the office of interpreting the Son to the "wondering" audience. Knowledge is introduced in a strangely off-hand way, to confirm the value of love: "well thou know'st how dear / To me are all my works." The Father then, informally but with precise detail, proceeds to unfold knowledge. One cannot speak with certainty upon such events, and the point I would suggest is a modest one, which I shall try to advance: that the easy fullness of the Father's exposition would not be inappropriate to foreknowledge responding to an occasion—or, indeed, responding, as only omniscience could, to an idea "from some other source." To isolate one desirable effect produced by that silent partnership of narrative and divine foreknowledge: the result is a general air and spirit of spontaneity, which is not one of the more familiar styles of omniscience.

In Book XI the basic situation is partly altered. The Son appears as "advocate," interpreting for man by applying general prediction to specific circumstances. The plea is that man be allowed to live "Before thee reconciled" and in peace. "All thy request was my decree," God answers, but without replying to the particular terms of the plea. Instead, the Father goes on to comment, more as judge than advocate, upon further conditions not brought forward by the Son. He announces the banishment from Paradise and declares death to be man's "final remedy." Reconciliation and peace would

seem to be reserved, as in the general language of Book III, for
the life after death, and only after a life

> *Tried in sharp tribulation, and refined*
> *By faith and faithful works, to second life.*
> *(XI, 63–64)*

Not until the middle of the stern behest to Michael does the
particularity of the Son's plea receive an answer. If—in addition to other terms of trial already on record—Adam and Eve
are patient in their obedience to Michael, they are to be dismissed "not disconsolate," "though sorrowing, yet in peace."
It is a direct answer to the advocate's plea for mitigation, but
not so acknowledged, and is delayed remarkably by other
business. An inexperienced advocate (or reader) might even
find himself thinking that the special point of the request had
become lost in the general decree.

Since God has established as decree all that the Son re-
quests, the Son's contribution, therefore, lies in his demonstrated love and free initiative. As in Book III, his freedom
expresses its perfection in God's will, inspired by love and
guided by reason. If we refer to the *Christian Doctrine*, we are
assured that a decree is to be understood "in the light
of . . . the condition upon which the decree depends." "So we
must conclude that God made no absolute decrees about anything which he left in the power of men, for men have freedom of action."[5]

In brief, God's extraordinary act of interpreting the Son in
Book III is repeated in Book XI—but now by the creation of a
dramatic stage and deliberate rhythm of presentation. By
withholding reference to peace and reconciliation, but
stressing death, banishment, and the continuation of human
trial, God emphasizes the place of "freedom of action" in
the fulfillment of His decree. He interprets—and silently
praises—the Son's example by choosing a dramatic form and
timing for the acceptance of the special plea. As Milton
writes the scene, God is Himself actor and author. At the
same time the cosmic gravity of a divine decree is staged
against a background which corresponds (by grace of divine
condescension) to the imaginative practices of human art.
God acts *as if* the plea for human reconciliation and peace
were won from Him, as if gradually after due reflection—

bringing into accord His decree, the Son's merit, and, one may add, an example of patient obedience.

Do these discriminations relieve the more troubling part of the Son's speech of any burden? I think not. When the Son attributes the fruits of penitential prayer to God's "implanted grace in man," but then pronounces on their superiority to the fruits of innocence, we are left in a state of doubt which does not seem to resemble the many deliberate, and stimulating, reticences of the poem. A ceremony of speech normal in addressing God suddenly moves from ceremony to purposive statement. Or does it? Is the expression by priest and advocate a figure of speech declared as a certainty but intended to assist the plea of reconciliation and peace? Or is it indeed a pronouncement—less perhaps the free action of validating a divine decree than the taking of initiative (as if from "some other source") to introduce the idea of transvaluing an evil event into a good, a good so desirable that its praise can dismiss with condescension the loss of that intermediate stage which preceded the evil?—

> On earth he first beheld
> Our two first parents, yet the only two
> Of mankind, in the happy garden placed,
> Reaping immortal fruits of joy and love,
> Uninterrupted joy, unrivaled love,
> In blissful solitude.
>
> (III, 64–69)

God accepts *all* of the Son's request, but then reveals further important conditions, and only after a definite sense of elapsed time indirectly acknowledges acceptance of the particular plea for reconciliation and peace. God says nothing on the judgment that concerns the fruits of innocence. The judgment must, however, accord with His will, obscure though the process may be, and is. In any event, God's silence does no particular good to the poem, and the judgment itself does harm—at least in the disorder retroactively released.

Milton's confident mastery of multiple analogies, with the delicate edge of mockery always turned at the precisely right angle, seems to lose an essential control and to tolerate embarrassing juxtapositions. The Son's pronouncement is not (except by the veil of doctrine) protected from comparison with the ambiguities of Adam's waking dreams—Adam's emphasis in preferring the Garden to his first view of the world outside and his responding to the first sight of Eve by a retrospective, radical devaluation of everything previously seen. Looking back one may find it not wholly unreasonable to ask—though the thought is painful—whether Adam was not a prophet unawares, perhaps anticipating the superior stage of penitence, in comparison with which everything previously experienced may be declared "mean." Even Adam's ominous transformation of Eve's beauty into the higher wisdom suggests a troubling range of similarity to the Son's pronouncement, and the cynical Satan may also have been, unawares and "aslope," the vehicle of prophecy:

> *O earth, how like to heav'n, if not preferred*
> *More justly, seat worthier of gods, as built*
> *With second thoughts, reforming what was old!*
> *For what God after better worse would build?*
> *(IX, 99–102)*

One may, I believe, register a disappointment where the poet has taught us to expect triumphs. For we have seen many examples of Milton's bold subtlety in risking fine lines that do not blur, that develop powerful tension in their closeness and similarity, and yet transfer that undiminished power to the solving clarity of convincing difference.

To conclude this part of the discussion, let us glance briefly at another rejection of the Garden:

> *then shall this mount*
> *Of Paradise by might of waves be moved*
> *Out of his place, pushed by the horned flood,*
> *With all his verdure spoiled and trees adrift*
> *Down the great river to the op'ning gulf,*
> *And there take root an island salt and bare,*
> *The haunt of seals and orcs, and sea-mews' clang:*
> *To teach thee that God attributes to place*
> *No sanctity, if none be thither brought*
> *By men who there frequent, or therein dwell.*
> *(XI, 829–38)*

The governing situations are of course different. Michael is presenting a prophetic vision, powerful and complete, and to Adam. The Son in Book XI is addressing God, and the reference to the Garden is only the most troubling item in the speech of priest and advocate. If the comparison of the two "rejections" has any value, it is to suggest why the poet behind Michael may still be thought to "sing with mortal voice unchanged."

An external cause, the Flood, does not hold back or divert the poet's own hand in the destruction of the Garden, though he is cancelling all the leisurely, loving amplitude that went into his creating and sustaining the image of the place. The sense of leisure is recapitulated, by a reflection as if subliminal, as the driving force of change spreads into a brief moment of drifting down toward the gulf which opens, and then Paradise itself is transformed and compressed into a couple of lines of "terrible beauty." Our own relation to the event thoroughly involves us in the sense of history, man's fate, and in these unimagined consequences vividly enacted, and in our own identification with the loving work destroyed. If we attribute our own human feelings to the poet, which his art of presence neither invites nor prevents, we shall find it difficult not to believe that his involvement resembles ours but is more deeply and intricately personal. He does not falter or fumble as we might do at the necessary task of imagining consequences. The austerity is extreme, that of the artist destroying his creation, but doing so by creating a miniature of unprecedented beauty, no less commanding than its imaginative opposite, the long moment of Mulciber's fall. The moral austerity is also humane, that of a mediator speaking to men "with mortal voice"—a hard task, fraught with the perils of privileged gloating, or self-hatred, or the secret flux of defensive sentiment, but a less hard task than that of composing the first speech of the first priest and advocate before God. The new conditions of life that justify the destruction of the Garden do not dismiss the sense of loss, and the new order is not declared to be better. The recognized contribution of human value is a consoling good, though a lesser good.

A major task of the last books is to reshape man in a new vision of order, but the poet's own fixed commitments assure continuity in the midst of change. There is no backing away from the primary laws of freedom, beginning with Adam's tortured monologue and the long trial of his capacity to learn the right lessons from the punishing instruction of Michael. Adam will stand "on even ground" once again; a major difference is that he will know and believe in his dependence on God, but he still must take responsibility for his acts. The experience of tragic failure will continue to be open to him, and the Paradise within is "happier far" at least in part because it is not immured by privilege. There still is no happiness without love, but in the new economy of joy love will have some further expression in "charity." The original purpose and need of love to provide solace will in no way be diminished. Adam's final definition of wisdom, though taught by the example of the Redeemer, and therefore with some additions, is based upon his earlier reply to the lecture on astronomy. If the first version seemed a little quick and easy, the second more than compensates by the painful slowness of its evolvement.

Some but not all of the apparent difficulties in the last books may be attributed to historical changes which have widened the distance between Milton's first and subsequent fit readers. I should not like to disqualify myself from that good company, but I wish to add that the resources of doctrine and history cannot show the validity of hope after failure by the same means that presented the demonstration of tragic failure; and, further, that dissatisfactions with the re-establishment of order in the poem are, to some extent, not unreasonable dissatisfactions with human destiny itself— and with official explanations which are not altogether free of the flawed human materials and history they explain. One may be willing to accept as a dignified necessity, but not as an unqualified improvement, the practical ethics of managing the Aristotelian mean. There may, however, be some reasonable reluctance to descend into that world from a Platonic world in which knowledge is tried and discovered by dialogue with a benign creator.

The principles of freedom endure in their tragic possibilities, and Milton is not willing to minimize the continuity of that emphasis. The poet who stood behind the figure of the Son expressing immortal love for the mortal carefully marked off the reservation of a potential difference and a potential denial: "above which only shone / Filial obedience." If the offer of sacrifice were not in accord with God's will, obedience would still shine. Both the Son as Mediator and the poet as mediator must be prepared to follow the truth of a denial and be willing to surrender everything else. If the limits are valid they must be obeyed. If they are disobeyed, established wisdom prescribes an educational descent into a state of personal darkness in order to find, to hold, and to value the human way back. The Son, as I have tried to argue, may go too far in praising the unqualified superiority of the first fruits of contrition, but the reality of "thou shalt not" is one of the necessary foundations of the poem. Adam redis-covers the value of saying no in his long monologue after the fall, and it is a turning point for him, away from Satan and toward God.

The issue has been present throughout the poem but kept from overshadowing the development of the story. Until Book IX human joy is natural and easy, like gratitude existing in a positive concord of intellect and will. When there is an occasion for saying no, however, the will cannot naturally produce a positive feeling of joy or gratitude. The obedient will can refuse to act against knowledge, but obedience must then be negative in posture and must practice the defense of denial, with some sacrifice of the otherwise desirable fruits of integrity in the expansiveness of joy. In the poem only the Son's expression of sacrifice creates a valid "Sense of new joy." The problem from this angle does not lend itself to satisfying comprehensive answers, but Milton thought the problem important enough to make the discriminating art of saying no a major subject of *Paradise Regained* and *Samson Agonistes*.

In heaven God—

> *Author of all being,*
> *Fountain of light, thyself invisible*
> *Amidst the glorious brightness where thou sitt'st*
> *Throned inaccessible, but when thou shad'st*
> *The full blaze of thy beams, and through a cloud*
> *Drawn round about thee like a radiant shrine,*
> *Dark with excessive bright. . . .*
> *(III, 374–80)*

—declares that "mercy first and last shall brightest shine." The "excessive bright" of the pronouncement will be made visible and will shine, but justice, the necessary middle term, will not shine. Yet justice is the point of balance between first and last, and the traditional symbolization of justice by the act of balancing is a "deep" figure, recognizable in the breath-ing downward of the Son's immortal love "To mortal men, above which only shone / Filial obedience." The figure of jus-tice is transfigured, as immortal love becomes the point of balance between the mortal and "Filial obedience." The free fulfillment of God's will is celebrated by the transfiguration, in which immortal love acts in the place of justice and filial

obedience shines as mercy. Adam, having discovered the first
negative steps in the isolation of his personal darkness, recovers his memory and his hope. He remembers the image of
his judge, and though the terms have been re-ordered in respect to time and place, *we* remember the original image seen
in heaven. Adam says:

> *Undoubtedly he will relent and turn*
> *From his displeasure; in whose look serene,*
> *When angry most he seemed and most severe,*
> *What else but favor, grace, and mercy shone!*
>
> *(X, 1093–96)*

What else but filial obedience?

Dismissed by Michael, Adam rushes to awaken Eve "but
found her waked," and the reader finds, through some mischief in the syntax, that he has mistaken who the speaker is
to be: "And thus with words not sad she him received." Adam
has had a full curriculum of vision, but she has had a dream
and wants to talk. We return suddenly to the he and she of
things, to a domestic scene reminiscent of Raphael's arrival.
Even the whimsicality of the syntax may remind us of the
artistic playfulness which is one indication of the poet's
normal presence.

Eve's speech is full of echoes, from this poem and from
others. It begins with some harmless egocentric chatter, then
moves to a mild display of satisfaction with her own direct
experience of knowledge in dreams, and then finally to a brief
statement that reminds us of the underlying reality of her
distress:

> *Whence thou return'st, and whither went'st,*
> *I know;*
> *For God is also in sleep, and dreams advise,*
> *Which he hath sent propitious, some great good*
> *Presaging, since with sorrow and heart's distress*
> *Wearied I fell asleep.*
>
> *(XII, 610–14)*

The pathos of her personal grief is transitional to the central
statement:

> *But now lead on;*
> *In me is no delay; with thee to go,*
> *Is to stay here; without thee here to stay,*

> *Is to go hence unwilling; thou to me*
> *Art all things under heav'n, all places thou,*
> *Who for my wilful crime art banished hence.*
> *(XII, 614–19)*

We hear a purified, strengthened revision of her evening love song; there is no dancing around Adam in an attractive display of herself and her responses; the *I* is without strain subordinated to the *thou*; the repetitions and contrasts are simple and strong. She does not forget to acknowledge her guilt and relate it to Adam's love. When she says, "thou to me / Art all things under heav'n," the last phrase quietly orders a great deal of troubled history into a final concord.

After this beautiful declaration of human love, the best statement in the poem and a long time in coming, Eve turns to the third and last part of her speech:

> *This further consolation yet secure*
> *I carry hence; though all by me is lost,*
> *Such favor I unworthy am vouchsafed,*
> *By me the Promised Seed shall all restore.*
> *(XII, 620–23)*

We hear the self-centeredness again, though chastened and humble and authorized, and we recall many details of her story, including her mild pride over the meal she intends to serve Raphael. Adam has learned some difficult lessons by which to master the life ahead; Eve is allowed to carry out of the Garden with her the consolation of personal hope. This is different in emphasis from her being the acknowledged vessel of religious hope, and a less generous poet could have easily refused to allow the emphasis. We should have missed something necessary then, perhaps without recognizing what it was.

Eve speaks in character as a voice of feeling, and expresses her share of the truth while permitting us to see more than she understands. It is her voice, but we have learned to recognize the characteristic interests and control of the poet behind the individual echoes, thematic advances, clarifications, and reticences. Her speech anticipates the great ending, with its measured balance of assured hope and assured grief as two human figures move simply away from our lost past and toward us in the indeterminate distance.

> *So spake our mother Eve, and Adam heard*
> *Well pleased, but answered not; for now too nigh*
> *Th' Archangel stood, and from the other hill*
> *To their fixed station, all in bright array*
> *The Cherubim descended.*
>   *(XII, 624–28)*

The poet marshals the evidence of time with convincing force and continues to do so until the pressure suddenly lets up in the last five lines of the poem. But the poet is, as he has been throughout, the sole master of timing. What may be said of Satan's implanted dream, or Adam's disclosure of passion, or Raphael's discourse on angelic love, may be said with minor qualifications of any episode in the poem: it is the poet alone who decreed the inclusion, the placement, the beginning, the order and emphasis of the content, and the termination. Whatever his obligations to the established content and significance of his materials, the poet has been responsible for wielding absolute authority over the external order of occurrence and the internal order of arrangement, and therefore over the secondary patterns of significance deriving from those relationships. To state Adam's reason ("for now too nigh") is to uncover its incompleteness. Like many statements in the poem, Adam's "reason" tells the truth of a narrative occasion while nodding suggestively in the direction of answers not given. No outside agency is needed to justify the human exchange of silence before the rush of action and the final lingering moment.

When Adam "answered not," the reader may refer to a treasury of answers we have heard throughout a long and eloquent poem. The negative is a small, shining affirmation of the work, divine and human, of justice and mercy. That the domestic house is in order, without which no paradise can be happy, is one of the unasked questions answered. The moment is a marvel of lightness, charm, surprise, and fulfillment. Adam's last individual act in the poem is, as it should be, perfect and unpredictable. In the pause created by the simple negative, poet, actors, and readers all meet and touch, variously, not disobeying the wisdom demonstrated by fable, the accomplishing of great things by small.

Notes

Introduction

1. *Complete Prose Works of John Milton* (New Haven: Yale University Press, 1953–74), II, 492–93. This edition will be cited hereafter as *C. P.*

2. Lorna Sage, "Milton in Literary History," in *John Milton: Introductions*, ed. J. B. Broadbent (Cambridge: Cambridge University Press, 1973), p. 340.

3. The chief contributions are those by Anne D. Ferry, *Milton's Epic Voice* (Cambridge; Harvard University Press, 1963) and by Louis L. Martz, *The Paradise Within* (New Haven: Yale University Press, 1964).

Chapter I. Beginnings: Speaking to the Poet

1. "Decay," *The Works of George Herbert*, ed. F. E. Hutchinson (Oxford: The Clarendon Press, 1941), p. 99.

2. Alfred North Whitehead, *Process and Reality* (New York: Macmillan, 1929), p. 7.

3. "Of Education," *C. P.*, II, 406. The quotation in the following sentence is from II, 403.

4. *C.P.*, II, 514–15.   5. *C.P.*, II, 493.   6. *C.P.*, II, 543.

7. Raphael's lecture on the scale of being quietly includes in that traditional hierarchical structure a small movement of radical import. The place on the scale is measured by the degree of nearness to God, "or nearer tending" (V, 476). A dynamic element is introduced which decreases the stability of rational prediction, exacts more strenuous efforts from the creature, and implies the constant condition of trial before the one judge who can know all the evidence, including the direction of the "tending." One may observe some resemblance between the angelic state and the inwardness of the spiritual striving by post-Reformation man.

8. As Raphael's exposition affirms, V, 409–13, 469ff. Cf. *C.P.*, VI, 309: "Moreover spirit, being the more excellent substance, virtually, as they say, and eminently contains within itself what is clearly the inferior substance; in the same way as the spiritual and rational

faculty contains the corporeal, that is, the sentient and vegetative faculty." Cf. note on the terms in *C.P.* and *P.L.*, VIII, 624.

9. That the language suggests Eve's demonic dream and the actual temptation may be construed in a deterministic way. I believe Milton's intention was more ambitious—that of bringing the morally neutral and the morally dangerous into open proximity, in order to emphasize their closeness and their separation.

Chapter II. Truth, Novelty, and Choice

1. The "erring" which he is about to straighten out in the punitive lines that follow also includes a witty rejection of his own inspired account.

2. *C.P.*, IV, 601.

3. In the previous example the expansion occurs between widely separated verbs partly abstract in their suggestiveness.

4. Medea's words from Ovid's *Metamorphoses*, VII, 11.20–21: "I see and approve the better and follow the worse." (I here borrow Douglas Bush's note on the passage.)

5. One is perhaps not straining unduly to detect in Adam's praise of passion a suggested devaluation of lesser joys in the concentrated exaltation of the single delight. Some latent tendency to disparage the good for the better may be implied in Adam's "wary speech" to Raphael, in which he thanks the guest for accepting "earthly fruits" as willingly as if "At heav'n's high feasts to have fed; yet what compare?" (V, 459–67)

6. Under the poet's guiding hand Satan will contribute to the humor of imagined correspondence between human and angelic love. In declaring himself on the standards of the "divinely fair, fit love for gods," Satan's absence from heaven (no less than the experience of hell and pain) seems to have "Enfeebled me, to what I was in heav'n" (IX, 488). He speaks of Eve's "heav'nly form / Angelic, but more soft and feminine" (IX, 457–78)—or rather, the narrative voice insinuates the words into the startled "pleasure" of Satan's consciousness. The epithets are at once the first mintage of enduring clichés and the nostalgic praise of pained memory, which is not what it was. To think of her form as "Angelic, but more soft" will require attributing to softness the quality of relative resistance—not difficult in the practices of human thought, but not easily reconciled with the conceptual standards appropriate for understanding angelic union as set forth by Raphael.

Chapter III. The Satanic Background

1. The difficulty is not unlike the common one of mastering the difference in meaning or idiom when the expression in a foreign language closely resembles an expression in one's native language.

2. Stanley Fish in *Surprised by Sin* (London and New York: Macmillan, 1967) has marshalled much of this evidence and argued his case with force and subtlety.

3. The exemplary issue of gratitude, intense, brief, and dramatic here, will apply indirect pressures to the story of Adam and Eve at a number of places.

4. In his long soliloquy in Book X Adam also goes through some of these movements.

5. I am echoing Sidney's *Defence of Poesie*, ed. Feuillerat in volume III of *The Complete Works* (Cambridge, 1923), pp. 14, 25. The deeper problems in Satan's attitude are visible but are not brought into a focus which permits useful analysis, though the fusing of divisions in the internal monologue does allow us to see the parts and where they are joined. To some extent the situation is thinking for Satan, as for a modern non-hero.

6. *Comus*, 207–08.

Chapter IV. The Story at the Center

1. The quotations from Spenser are in his letter to Sir Walter Raleigh prefixed to *The Faerie Queene;* the reference to Sidney is in *The Defence of Poesie*, ed. Feuillerat, III, 20.

2. Cf. Cleanth Brooks, "Eve's Awakening," in *Essays in Honor of W. C. Curry* (Nashville: Vanderbilt University Press, 1954), pp. 281–98.

3. In the hymn of Book V the things of nature are seen with a minimal admixture of the observers' personal presence. Eve's song, like her first narcissistic experience, the demonic dream, and the temptation itself, all tend to direct what is other and external toward what is herself and internal.

4. I am indebted to the discussion by Thomas Kranidas, *The Fierce Equation* (The Hague: Mouton, 1965), pp. 145–54.

5. For the domestic scene Milton would appear to allow himself more liberal use of the foreground of future experience than customary. But the scene is a special one which entertains far more than it threatens.

6. Irene Samuel's influential interpretation of the dialogue in heaven as drama (*PMLA*, LXXII, 1957, 601–11) opens on the scene a critical door which can be further opened or closed but has also encouraged in others a certain rash knocking down of walls.

7. See, for instance, Barbara Lewalski's noteworthy analysis, "Innocence and Experience in Milton's Eden," *New Essays on Paradise Lost*, ed. Thomas Kranidas (University of California Press, 1969), p. 102. To which I may add two substantial older studies: W. B. Hunter, "Eve's Demonic Dream," *ELH*, XIII (1946), 255–65; Howard Schultz, "Satan's Serenade," *P.Q.*, XXVII (1948), 17–26. A recent ambitious effort to reinterpret the episode is that of Dan S. Collins,

"The Buoyant Mind in Milton's Eden," *Milton Studies*, V (1973), 229–48.

The literature on dreams is immense, but we may assume that Milton had a grasp of the options open to him. Since Eve's dream is inspired by Satan, the dream itself, though not the dreamer, would come under the general class of postlapsarian demonic dreams. There is no suggestion of that current, preromantic fancy that the slumber of the body is the waking of the soul. (One reservoir of the thought presents it with a necessary, systematic seriousness: to Plotinus, III, vi, 6, the world of sense may be figured as "the soul in its slumber; for all of the soul that is in body is asleep. . . the veritable waking or rising is from corporeal things. . . .") It should be safe to assume that Milton accepted the conservative rational opinion, that though the will is powerless in its unconscious state and can be inclined, it cannot be forced; demons can corrupt only those who accept their evil.

Plainly there are problems, and Milton did not try, too hard, to resolve them for the sake of theory. To have denied any effect of the dream would have been to admit the superfluousness of Raphael's embassy. On the other hand, he cannot and would not intimate that Eve accepted the evil of the dream, and he refuses to provide hard details that would clearly indicate the influence of the dream upon subsequent events—which he might easily, or even carelessly, have done. The dream remains ambiguous, the matter of trial, though "infused" from without, a major strain upon the weaker vessel, whose nature is less fully developed by the story and is for that reason (among others) more fit to initiate the mysterious origin of human sin. Part of the ambiguity of the dream lies in its formal neutrality, an invasion from without that cannot itself command the will. In this respect Eve's experience belongs to the general category of Adam's waking dreams.

8. There are reticences in the dialogue also, or, rather, a kind of openness and drift which some critics have accepted as a direct invitation to "complete" the story. Some of the invested complexity of love, as in the conditions of yielding and receiving, is here brought into direct collision with the necessary freedom to judge and choose. One cannot think that Milton's invention and narrative management of the scene over-rationalizes this step in the direction of the mysterious origin of sin. As in the narrative choice of gratitude, or the state of dream and waking dream, the poet (putting the theologian behind him) exploits the capacities of fiction to negotiate "darkness visible" and emerge from indistinct causes with clear effects, and by means of a process that is so convincing in itself that it may seem bad-mannered ingratitude to insist that he show cause. The atmosphere of passivity and drift is itself foreboding, and not only because of ancient associations of passivity and evil. The governing principles of the universe appear to allow no legitimate room

for such. Like the indistinct music of Pandemonium, what happens without conscious agent, or is accepted without conscious choice, would seem to be part of the matter of "magic"—to which the only adequate answer may be calm trust in God, the treasure most likely to be the aim, or the trial, of circumstances not clearly understood. As in the pages touching on the problem of the "hidden God" and the limits of knowledge (see pp. 145–46), I am here trying to indicate a border region that Milton accepted and needed for his story but had little inclination to explore.

9. See John Dixon Hunt, *The Figure and the Landscape* (Baltimore: Johns Hopkins University Press, 1976), Chapter I.

10. There is, I think, a certain tenacious ambiguity concerning the pleasures of solitude. Though Adam's problem is to imagine Eve's feelings, contemplation is the attribute that properly belongs to his nature. As with the compressed syntax of "absents thee more," which, if completed, would have to acknowledge the prominent effect of her absence, not only on her but on him, the thought of Eve's potential desire for solitude does not seem to be directed toward her without regard to the possibilities of solitude for himself. Adam cannot quite imagine Eve as a being separate from himself, and she feels an undefined urge to establish her separateness. The pattern has modern and primitive analogues, domestic and metaphysical. One suspects that in private conversation Milton could have defined these matters with some precision, and could have cited the philosophical, esoteric, and personally observed sources. In the poem, however, he prefers to avoid the rigidities of translating some kinds of imaginative knowledge into wisdom for daily use.

11. Fredson Bowers leads the way, with his characteristic delight in combining scholarly information and the austerely detached logic of a textual critic accustomed to making clean decisions. See "Adam, Eve, and the Fall in *Paradise Lost*," *PMLA*, LXXXIV (1969), 264–73; and further: Deane K. McColley, "Free Will and Obedience in the Separation Scene of *Paradise Lost*," *SEL*, VII (1972), 103–20; Stella P. Revard, "Eve and the Decline of Responsibility in *Paradise Lost*," *PMLA* LXXXVIII (1973), 69–78.

12. Comprehensive though *Paradise Lost* is, it is also selective and does not attempt to do everything equally. The best readers have always known this, but the poem is so powerful that an occasional reminder ought to be tolerated. That "man" means "man and woman" in the more philosophical interpretations of *Genesis* does not quite cover all matters. Milton makes a considerable effort, analytical and imaginative, to represent the two great sexes as composing one human nature, the virtues and defects of which are intricately intertwined. But the task of the narrative artist, no less than that of the theologian, requires that Adam alone bear the full weight of a tragic protagonist. The poet does well by Eve, much better than the inherited materials and traditions of interpretation would seem

to promise, but he is bound by the choices he makes in the development of his story. There is no conceivable possibility, for instance,
that he could emulate Shakespeare's dazzling invention of an emerging tragic role for Cleopatra. The argument that justifies the ways of
God to men is directed toward the rational endowment of human
nature, the understanding of which has never been without problems. Milton's answers, however noble or true, cannot dispossess,
dissolve, or foreclose the renewable claims of such problems on
human interest. In any case, it is plain that he does not offer, or think
himself in any way obliged to, a special justification of God's ways to
women. I am more than a little diffident toward the evidence Northrop Frye musters in a strenuous and fascinating essay, "The Revelation to Eve," in *Paradise Lost: A Tercentenary Tribute*, ed. B.
Rajan (Toronto, 1969). But his last sentence is indeed memorable,
even if the life it generates appears to draw but a special and tangen-
tial impulse from the Eve of Milton's poem: "We are expected to be
similarly convicted and convinced, but, if the clear light of reason is
ever dimmed by a passion or emotion that is not quite so sure of its
objects, we may remember that, far below this rarefied pinnacle of
rational vision, there lies a humiliated mother dreaming of the vengeance of her mighty son."

13. See Harold E. Toliver, "Complicity of Voice in Paradise Lost,"
M.L.Q., XXV (1964), 153–70.

14. I owe this observation to my student, Mark Crispin Miller.

15. Adam's rapt horror before he broke "inward silence" may
suggest some glancing resemblance to Satan giving birth to Sin. Less
glancing is the resemblance of one effect: the desperate raciness that
fills Adam's speech soon afterward echoes the reception accorded
Sin once she has "familiar grown." She "pleased."

16. The statement serves no ulterior purpose of self-deception,
though we cannot tell whether the "cursed fraud" expresses judgment, imprecation, or angry resignation. We may have similar doubt
concerning "now to death devote."

17. The progressive systematizing of Platonic thought tended to
bridge and assign a dominant function to all discoverable interstices.
Thus Plotinus: "The will of any organic thing is one; but the distinct
powers which go to constitute it are far from being one. . . . Right
will, then, the will which stands above accidental experience, seeks
The Good and thus acts to the same end with it" (IV, iv, 35). And
thus Hooker in denying that the will proper is involved in any desire
"unless reason prescribeth" *(Ecclesiastical Polity*, I, vii, 3). One may
apply these definitions retrospectively to Adam's case, and add Calvin's radical departure from Socratic ethics *(Institutes*, II, ii, 23) and
the *Nicomachean Ethics* (VII, iii), the thesis that incontinence
rushes into sin knowingly without the excuse of a false good. Milton
might well have recognized some of the advantages of such abrupt-
ness for the crucial moment of his story, but he could hardly have

subscribed to the definition, which prefers Tertullian to Socrates and posits a corrupt and equal partnership of will and intellect. Adam's love for Eve is a good, a divinely sanctioned good and not a false good, and certainly not a part of some "accidental experience." Nor is Adam "unknowing" in any common way. As Milton tells the story Adam's case is a dense and comprehensive simplicity, the meanings of which will yield themselves to reasoning, whether systematic or intermittent, and the reasoning is in less danger of being altogether wrong than of being partial and incomplete.

18. That is, the series has a paradigmatic correctness, though the context indeed stimulates a sense that the expression is problematical. The effect is not one of Milton's lesser surprises, and we may be reminded further that an incorrect version of the paradigm has been latent at least since Book VIII—one in which Eve potentially threatens to become the source whence Adam's good, not descends but ascends.

This may be a convenient place to record some other surprises— briefly and informally, without attempting to describe their intricacies. In Eve's temptation all her argument is with God; not until after her violation does she think of Adam. In Adam's temptation all of his argument in effect is with Eve; he thinks until the last moment, but not of God. One may add a similar observation: at the crisis Adam's "visual" contemplation, which characteristically moves outward to build upon the external, begins to resemble a tendency more characteristic of Eve, to direct what is other toward herself. That delicate equilibrium of passivity in love—yielding and receiving—is broken, and Adam turns into a kind of second-best receiver of what is not truly yielded. He is overcome by "female charm" not literally but symbolically and comprehensively, as he "approves" his acceptance of transposed roles. Within the limits of innocence Milton, among other "things unattempted," manages to discover some kinds of trial "by what is contrary."

Chapter V. The Art of Presence

1. Her "first thoughts" are remarkably well ordered. If Adam agrees to divide their labors, Eve has two general and two specific suggestions to offer him. One statement will cover her plans.

2. I think particularly of B. Rajan, who traces the "blossoming" of the images from the "seed of repentance" to "the tree of redemption" : *The Lofty Rhyme* (London: Routledge and Kegan Paul, 1970), pp. 86–87.

3. *C.P.*, VI, 555–56.

4. *C.P.*, VI, 162–63.

5. *C.P.*, VI, 155.

Index

Adam, discussed in major episodes: disclosure of passion, 54 ff.; introduction of, 91 ff.; debate on separation, 110 ff.; the fall, 123 ff.; after penitential prayer, 137 ff.; "answered not," 177. *See also* Dreams; Freedom; Trial

Auditory images: of Adam, 95, 98, 100, 119 f.; of Eve, 95; in heaven, 90, 97; remembered, 90, 175

Aristotelian ethics, 173, 184

Background: Milton's deliberate construction of, 54 ff., 61, 65, 68 f., 103, 125, 128, 131; and reader, 85; indistinctly controlled, 111 ff.; of Satan immobilized, 148 f. *See also* Foreground; Satan

Balance: and Milton's design, 89–91; and human love, 91, 135; and divine love, 174 f. *See also* Imbalance

Beginnings: and first principles, 14 f., 17 f., 19 f.; of tragic experience, 115

Bowers, Fredson, 183

Bush, Douglas, 180

Calvin, John, 184

Choice: revealed in language, 34; and denial, 59, 131, 173–175, 177; in Paradise, 113

Collins, Dan S., 181 f.

Dialogue: and argument, 31; and the discovery of human love, 54; Socratic prototype, 111 f., 143; of love, 132

Dreams: Adam's waking dreams, 21–27; related to disclosure of passion, 60; Eve's demonic dream, 103–110; its ambiguity, 104, 182; and narrative method, 108;

"rehearsal" of fall, 121; and knowledge, 175

Eve: introduction of, 91–97; love song, 97–99; temptation, 121–123; and Adam compared, 139; her elaborate departure, 153–156; her last speech, 175 f.; as "tragic accomplice," 183 f.

Ferry, Anne D., 179

Fish, Stanley E., 181

Foreground: problems of, 52, 67; and the reader, 68, 115; relaxation of, 117, 181n5; after the fall, 132. *See also* Background

Foreknowledge: and the reader, 85; God's, 86, 168; and established rules of story, 89, 126; and the scene of domestic tension, 98 f.; of narrative artist, 120, 146; and "suggestions," 127–129. *See also* Freedom

Freedom: and continuity, 16, 18 f., 172 f.; principles of, 2, 28, 91; moral rules of in poem, 23, 26, 104, 110, 114, 127; related to understanding, 43, 54 f., 110, 113, 117; and reader, 68; and innocence, 107; domestic model of, 114 f.; of Adam in crisis, 121; the poet's venturing beyond the rules, 152; celebrated, 174 f. *See also* Choice; Poet; Trial

Frye, Northrop, 184

Gratitude: and joy, 55 f., 59, 174; and knowledge, 55–59; and Satan, 69–71; and "responding," 91; in a domestic scene, 101

Herbert, George, 13, 72

Hooker, Richard, 184

187

Index of Quotations

190